COMMENT

"Missy breaks your heart, ̶ ̶ ̶ ̶ ̶ ̶ ̶ ̶ ̶ ̶ ̶, and makes you a believer—in f̶ ̶ ̶ ̶ ̶, faith, and how the strength of one girl can change the world."

Diane Sawyer, ABC News
Good Morning America

꧁◦꧂

"Through Missy's narrative, you'll learn how this young woman moved from being part of a headline...to being an inspiration. Thank you, Missy, for showing us the healing qualities of forgiveness and real grace in the face of adversity."

Robin Meade, CNN Headline News
Morning Express with Robin Meade

꧁◦꧂

"Missy Jenkins is more than a survivor. She is living testimony to the fact that a loving family and a supportive community bring forth the best in someone who has been hurt beyond measure. Those inner qualities of resilience, determination, optimism, and empathy flourish in Missy. Her life is full of joy and meaning and she has become a symbol of courage for the thousands of young people who have seen her on television and learned from her example. Rampage school shootings are, thankfully, very rare. But they are devastating to their victims, including the innocent bystanders who cannot forget what they have witnessed. Understandably, we dwell on the horror and the sadness.

"What this book shows us is that in this rare case, it is possible to do more than go on. For Missy, the shooting has provided a purpose in life: to help young people who are misunderstood, angry and roiling inside, to reach out to them with sympathy in the hopes that they will never feel so isolated as her assailant, Michael Carneal, did so many years ago. This book has a great deal to teach us all."

Katherine S. Newman, Forbes Class of 1941 Professor of Sociology and Public Affairs, Princeton University and senior author of *Rampage: The Social Roots of School Shootings*

"Missy shares her inspiring story of life after tragedy with candor and vulnerability. She tells of how she chose hope over despair and has discovered purpose, strength and the grace to use the atrocity at her high school as a catalyst to becoming a person determined to change the world! Missy is a woman of great passion and character, who has the ability to inspire all people to live each moment to the fullest, and embrace the life they have been given. Her pursuit of God and forgiveness will undoubtedly touch your heart so deeply that you will forever be changed after reading this book!"

Crystal Woodman Miller
Columbine High School shooting survivor, Speaker,
Author of *Marked for Life*

❧

"This is a story everyone should know. It is about a remarkable young lady overcoming tremendous adversity to find happiness and fulfillment. But it is also about something much more universal in its appeal and its need. It is about hope - how one person, through hard work, an indomitable will and a luminescent spirit, really can change the world. Missy Jenkins inspires me, and I know she will do the same for anyone fortunate enough to read this book."

Dan Gross, CEO and Co-founder
PAX / Real Solutions to Gun Violence

❧

"As a 15 year old who had just been shot and paralyzed, Missy Jenkins showed a maturity well beyond her years by immediately accepting her fate and adapting to life as a paraplegic. Her determination, strength and bravery shine through this book, which offers valuable lessons to people of all ages."

Jim Abbott
Former major league pitcher

I Choose to be Happy

I Choose to be Happy

A School Shooting Survivor's
Triumph Over Tragedy

By Missy Jenkins
with William Croyle

LANGMARC
PUBLISHING
Austin, Texas

I Choose to Be Happy
A School Shooting Survivor's Triumph Over Tragedy
by Missy Jenkins with William Croyle

Cover layout: Michael Qualben
Cover photograph: Patrick Reddy

Scripture quotations are from the
King James Version, Revised
of the *Holy Bible*

Published by LangMarc Publishing
P.O. 90488
Austin, TX 78709
www.langmarc.com

Library of Congress Control Number 2008932555

ISBN: 1-880292-319

Dedication

FROM MISSY

To Josh and Logan,
    You mean so much to me, have been there for me
    and believed in me every step of the way.
        I love you both.

To my mom, dad and siblings,
        You put your lives on hold to make sure
            I could keep living mine.
        I love you, and thank you so much!

FROM WILLIAM

To Debra,
    Your guidance, wisdom, and love made this happen.
        Thank you for being my wife and best friend.

To my boys,
    May this book inspire you to never quit chasing your
    dreams, no matter what obstacles you may face.

CONTENTS

Foreword

Life couldn't have been better for Jim and me. We'd been married nearly nine years, had a beautiful two-year-old son, and Jim's new job as White House press secretary under President Ronald Reagan was a dream come true. But it took just a split second – and a deranged man with a gun – to crush that dream. In an assassination attempt on our nation's leader, John Hinckley Jr. shot four people on March 30, 1981: the President, Jim, a Secret Service agent and a police officer.

Jim was the most seriously injured with a bullet lodged in his brain. He underwent an emergency five-hour surgery that day, and several more surgeries over the course of the year. When he finally left the hospital after eight months, he was unable to use his left arm or left leg, had trouble speaking, faced years of strenuous therapy and suffered from a great deal of physical pain that is still with him today.

But through it all Jim has never complained about his situation, has always put his trust in the Lord and has worked hard at turning a tragic situation into something good. It was Jim's attitude that enabled him to regain control of his life and make a difference in the lives of others. It's the same attitude possessed by Missy Jenkins.

I was sitting in my office at the Brady Center to Prevent Gun Violence in Washington, D.C., on December 1, 1997, when I heard the news about a school shooting at Heath High School in Paducah, Kentucky. Such violence in schools was rare back then compared to today, but was happening with more frequency. Three young, innocent girls – Nicole Hadley, Jessica James and Kayce Steger – were shot and killed by their schoolmate, 14-year-old Michael Carneal. Five other students were injured, including Missy.

Paralyzed from the chest down, Missy faced the rest of her life in a wheelchair. She had to learn the basics all over again, such as getting herself in and out of bed, putting on her clothes and simply getting from one place to another. But like Jim, she has never complained about her situation, has trusted in the Lord's plan for her and has created a lot of good from that tragedy.

Jim and Missy could have chosen to live the rest of their lives in seclusion, feeling sorry for themselves and hiding their disabilities from the world. But they felt they had a responsibility to turn what happened to them, their friends and colleagues into something from which future generations could learn and benefit. And they've done just that.

I see two common denominators in nearly every shooting: the shooter is someone who had easy access to a gun, and is someone who is mentally troubled.

In regard to the former denominator, Jim and those of us associated with the Brady Center have made great strides in creating a safer America with the passing of the Brady Bill in 1993, and several legislative efforts to hold adults responsible for keeping their guns out of the hands of children.

Missy, meanwhile, has successfully focused on the latter denominator. She strives each day to reach people in distress through her full-time job of counseling troubled teens at a day treatment center. It's a career she chose so she could help those who may be on the same devastating path Michael Carneal was on. She also regularly gives talks at schools, teaching children to make good choices and to take responsibility for what they do.

And now, this courageous young woman has chosen to share her story in remarkable detail through this poignant book. From the day she was shot to the day she met face to face with her shooter a decade later, Missy will take you on her incredible journey of sorrow, pain, joy and triumph. Some may read this and simply realize that her plight can put a bad day in perspective. Others may be able to relate to the more complex lessons she offers, such as the importance of forgiving the one who hurt you the most. But one thing is certain – there's a lesson in here for everyone, young and old.

I hope you enjoy – and learn from – Missy's story.

Sarah Brady

ACKNOWLEDGEMENTS

One thing we've learned about writing a book is that it takes the contributions and cooperation from countless people over several years to make it happen. Thank you to everyone who helped us along the way. We would especially like to recognize:

From Missy:

Josh, for the love and patience you bring to our marriage every day, and for the sacrifices you make in taking care of our family. Logan, my light and inspiration who teaches me something new each day. My parents, Ray and Joyce Jenkins – you've been by my side every moment, always making sure I've had the best possible care; I wouldn't have made it without you. And all of my siblings, for your love and sacrifice in making sure your baby sister not only survived, but prospered in every way possible.

From William:

Debra, for unconditionally supporting everything I do; you are the reason for my successes. My boys – you make me proud every day. My mom and dad, Jean and Bill Croyle – you taught me to love, laugh, have faith and serve others; thank you for all you've given me. My sister, Lynne Stark; my grandmothers; and all of my relatives and friends who have supported me in this endeavor. My niece and goddaughter, Madelyn, the bravest little girl I know. And my grandfathers – I miss you both.

From Missy and William:

Those who so graciously edited our work, each giving us a unique perspective: Pam McQueen, Leslie Hughes, Garri Hunt, Christi Geary, Brian Geary, Debra Croyle and the students in the class of 2008 at St. Joseph School in Crescent Springs, Kentucky.

The wonderful people of Paducah who were kind enough to share their stories, documents, photos and other information from that fateful day: Kenya Atherton, Dianne Beckman, Bill Bond, Susie Carroll, Duke Conover, Mary Camille Dummer, Pam Hale, Kelly Alsip, Sheriff Jon Hayden, Mandy Jenkins, Tim Kaltenbach, Christie Starner and Russ Tilford.

Ronald Goldfarb and Lois Qualben, who believed in us and took a chance on us. Thank you for your faith and guidance in our work.

Sarah and James Brady. You're an inspiration. We admire your strength and courage. Thank you for sharing it with us.

Diane Sawyer, Robin Meade, Katherine S. Newman, Dan Gross, Crystal Woodman Miller and Jim Abbott: thank you all so much for your kind words of support.

Dennis Repenning and Sid Easley, who managed our legal interests so we could concentrate on writing. You handled everything with the utmost confidence and professionalism, giving us one less thing to worry about.

Patrick Reddy. Your photos are the best of the best. Thank you for making us look good. And Lisa Stamper and Hannah Wagner – your technological prowess is unmatched. Thank you all for your creativity and hard work.

The many long-time friends and those we met along this journey who contributed in ways, big and small, that helped us reach our destination: Patrick Crowley, Karen Gutiérrez, Kristen Korian, Lilly Walters, Ryan Clark, Roger Palmer, Dr. David Grimes, Alan Mullins, Harry Allison, LuAnn McLane, Patsy Swendson and Noonie Fortin.

And those who made possible the historic visit with Michael Carneal. The wounds will never fully heal, but the meeting was certainly a step in the right direction: David Harshaw, Tim Arnold, Linda Harvey, Jeff From, Paige McGuire, John Rees, Larry Chandler, Sarah, Kelly and Michael.

"...we must redouble our efforts to protect all our children from violence and make sure our schools are free from violence and the means to wreak it."
— President Bill Clinton
December 2, 1997

1

THREE DEAD, FIVE INJURED

"Like all Americans, I was shocked and heart-broken by the terrible news, which I followed very closely when it broke. Of course, we still don't know all the facts surrounding the tragedy or why a 14-year-old boy would take a pistol and open fire on his classmates in a prayer group. We may never know, but we must redouble our efforts to protect all our children from violence and make sure our schools are free from violence and the means to wreak it. I believe that I speak for every American in sending our thoughts and prayers to the parents of Kayce Steger, Jessica James, Nicole Hadley and the wounded children and the entire community of West Paducah."
—President Bill Clinton, December 2, 1997[1]

As a 15 year old, like many my age, I had the attitude that I was invincible. Nothing could hurt me. It didn't matter what I did, or where or with whom I was. Untimely tragedy and death only happened to other

1

people in faraway places. A good example was Pearl, Mississippi, the site of one of the nation's first school shootings. It was October 1, 1997, at Pearl High School, 400 long miles south of my peaceful hometown of West Paducah, Kentucky. A 16-year-old student from Pearl named Luke Woodham entered the building early that morning and callously fired his hunting rifle, killing two classmates and leaving seven students injured.[2]

School shootings are all too common today, but they were a rarity back then. In fact, the Pearl shooting received extensive media coverage for weeks because such an act was so unusual. I read about it in newspapers and on the Internet. I watched video clips on every television station. It was all that anybody talked about, but that was as close as it got to me. I'd never even heard of the town until then, and I certainly didn't know anybody there. Nothing like that could ever happen here, I thought. It was far removed from my quiet life.

But at about 7:40 A.M. on December 1, 1997, just two months to the day after the Pearl tragedy, I found out how naive I was through a firsthand, boorish lesson in mortality. A 14-year-old freshman in my school named Michael Carneal, a classmate I knew, liked, and even admired, casually entered through the back door of Heath High School with a blanket full of guns and an olive-colored backpack loaded with shells and a gun.[3] He calmly made the long, winding trek through the band room, auditorium, and back hallways until he reached the small, crowded, front lobby where scores of students were gathered before classes began. He put the blanket of guns down, reached into his backpack, pulled out a .22-caliber semi-automatic pistol, and opened fire.

It was supposed to be an ordinary Monday for me. I had a first-period world civilization test to take that I had studied for over the long Thanksgiving holiday weekend we'd just concluded. Michael and I were supposed to have band practice together later that day, as we did every day. And I was looking forward to catching up with my best friend, Kelly Hard, whom I hadn't seen since the previous week.

But none of that happened.

This photo appeared in the *Paducah Sun* on Dec. 2, 1997. It's probably the most recognized photo from the shooting, having been picked up by the Associated Press and appearing in publications nationwide. (*Paducah Sun*/Steve Nagy)

Instead, I witnessed 14-year-old freshman Nicole Hadley, one of Michael's friends and one of the nicest girls in the school, fall helplessly to the floor after Michael shot her in the head. She was the first one hit as she stood in the middle of the lobby, only a few feet from him. Nicole died that night.[4]

I watched 17-year-old senior Jessica James, another sweet girl with such a bright future, go into violent convulsions next to me after he shot her below the left shoulder, piercing a main artery. Jessica fought valiantly to survive, but lost her battle. She died later that morning.[5]

Sophomore Kayce Steger, 15, had a dream of becoming a police officer. She was one of my friends and another of Michael's fatal victims. Kayce was near me, on the opposite side of the lobby from Michael. She had her back to him and was likely running away from him when the shots were fired. She was just a step or two from being shielded by a cinder-block pillar, but a bullet caught up with her, hitting her in the back of the head. She was pronounced dead about 45 minutes later.[6]

Wounded were my friend, Kelly Hard, 16; Shelley Schaberg, 17; Craig Keene, 15; Hollan Holm, 14; and me.

My limp, paralyzed body lay on the cold, hard, tile floor of the lobby just seconds after praising God in our daily prayer circle. I lay there helplessly on my back, staring straight up at the ceiling. I couldn't feel my legs or stomach. I could barely move my head. And I had no idea why. Chaos ensued around me as dozens of students with ear-piercing screams dashed out of the lobby and stampeded down the hallway toward the gymnasium, trying to save themselves. At the same time, several teachers bravely fought their way toward the lobby against the mad rush of terrified teens, trying to reach me and the others who needed help.

This must have been what Pearl was like, except I wasn't reading about it or watching it on television. This wasn't 400 miles away. It was happening here in my tightly-knit school of about five hundred students, where everybody knew and trusted each other. It was happening here in West Paducah, a small, rural, serene Ohio River town where not a whole lot ever happened. We liked it that way. But that innocence was lost in about ten seconds with Michael's rampage. He killed three. He physically injured five. He psychologically wounded not just our whole community, but an entire nation. It's difficult for anybody, even today, to think of our city without referring to what commonly became known as "the Paducah school shooting."

As the chaos inside Heath continued that fateful morning, the 7:45 A.M. bell rang as it always did to begin the school day. A few students were lingering in the lobby, doing whatever they could to try to help us. Some were in their classrooms, still oblivious to the devastation. Most had been herded into the gym as a safe haven. As for me, I was supposed to be in my world civilization class taking that test. Instead, I was on the floor, powerless, wondering if I was about to die.

Before I'd even arrived at school, the day had gotten off to a pretty dismal start. Sluggish, I awoke about 6 o'clock that morning to my dad's daily, maddening wake-up call. My twin sister, Mandy, and I shared a room in our small, three-bedroom ranch home. Dad would always come in and feverishly shake her bed because it would make a rattling noise. As if that weren't enough to irritate us, he'd belt out a really annoying song at the top of his lungs. "It's time to get up, it's time to get up, it's time to get up in the morning," he'd sing.

I love my dad so much, but I remember always being so irritated when he would go through that ritual. That day was no different.

I was coming off what had started as a fantastic holiday weekend. I spent Thanksgiving Day with my parents and all five of my siblings, helped put up the Christmas tree on Friday, and spent time with some friends on Saturday. But on Sunday things turned sour between my mom, Mandy, and me. Mom asked and expected me to go to church with her that morning, but I decided instead to go see *Anastasia* at the theater with some friends. Then I had the nerve to call Mom when the movie was over and ask if one of my friends could come over. After the church snub, there was no way she was going to allow that.

The day worsened when Mandy and I got home and fought over which of us got to use the Internet, a relatively new phenomenon to us at the time. What started as a shouting match turned into an all-out brawl with hitting, scratching, and even biting. Mom finally got fed up with our antics and grounded us. With nothing left to do, we went to bed.

When we woke up the next morning, the sun hadn't yet risen, the four-day weekend of fun was over, Dad was bellowing the same old tune, school was back in session, and it was supposed to be a cold, gloomy day. An ominous combination.

I usually dressed up for school but was way too lazy to fix myself up that day. I took a quick shower and put on some makeup, but that was as much effort as I was going to put into my appearance. I threw on a pair of black Adidas sweatpants, a white long-sleeved shirt that belonged to a friend, and a black Adidas shirt over that. Like any kid who has to go to school coming off of a holiday weekend, I had no sense of urgency whatsoever. Realizing that I was running late, I frantically put my hair in a ponytail, ate a Pop Tart, slipped on my tennis shoes, and headed for the front door. Mom and Dad were in their bedroom.

"We're leaving," I yelled. They didn't respond, but I was pretty sure they heard me. We were late and had no time for hugs or kisses. I never even thought about an "I love you." We had to go. We'd see them when we got home.

Mandy and I had gotten over our argument from the previous day and were back on good terms with each other. Whenever we would fight, it would never last long at all. We were twins, inseparable all our lives, and never held grudges toward each other. It was just assumed that what happened had happened and was a thing of the past.

We rode to school that day, as we did every day, with our friend, Taylor Garland, who lived two doors down from us. Taylor was a freshman that year, but her older sister, Carrie, was a senior with a car. We left between 7:15 and 7:20. It was an uneventful ride. The radio was on and nobody said much. School was only 15 minutes away, and I was hoping we'd make it in time for the prayer circle, which usually started around 7:35.

I first saw the prayer circle the year before as a freshman. There weren't that many kids in it then, so I didn't really pay much attention to it. In this, my sophomore year, it had grown considerably to about 35 students. One of my friends who was in it told me I could join them if I wanted, so I decided to try it. Having grown up believing in God and having been baptized less than two years earlier, the prayer circle was something I ended up looking forward to each day before school. Prayer was important to me. I had prayed often as a child and relied on prayer to get me through some difficult times, including health problems encountered by my mom, dad and oldest sister, Pam. I don't know how I would have made it through those times without prayer.

The prayer circle was massive, extending around the entire lobby. We joined hands and a student leader in the group would call on people who wanted to make prayer requests. Some would pray for sick friends or family members. Others might have prayed for something more global, such as peace on earth. It would go on for a couple minutes, maybe less. The leader would then say a prayer and we'd all say amen. After that, we'd break apart and chat for a minute before going to class. It was a comforting way to start our day.

When we got to school that Monday morning, Carrie and Taylor went straight to class. Mandy and I hooked up with Kelly in the lobby and stayed there for the prayer circle. We got there right when it started, but I wasn't feeling well. I don't know what was wrong, but my body just didn't feel right. I wanted to go to the bathroom but didn't want to go alone. I asked Kelly to go with me.

"Let's just do the prayer circle, and we'll go to the bathroom afterwards," she said. I decided that was fine. No big deal. I could wait a few minutes. But I've always wondered why I didn't just ask Mandy to go with me. She was my sister and best friend in the world. She was right there with me but, for whatever reason, I didn't

Heath High School is one of three high schools in the McCracken County School District.

The lobby today looks just as it did before the shooting occurred. This is a view from where Michael was standing when he fired the shots. I was standing by the plant in the background on the left. Nicole Hadley was standing near the desk. Jessica James was in front the pillar on the left, where the pirate now stands.

This is the view from where I was standing when I was shot. Michael was in front of the trophy case to the right.

You can see again where I was and where Jessica James was when the shots were fired. This view shows the hall students ran down to escape the gunfire. They ran out those double doors and to the gym. Kayce Steger was heading down that hallway and was just to the left of the pillar near the pirate when she was shot.

ask. It's fascinating how even the smallest choices we make, such as whether or not to go to the bathroom at a certain time, can affect the direction of our entire lives. Had I gone, I probably would have missed the prayer circle – and Michael's rage.

The lobby was rectangular – about 50 feet wide by 25 feet deep as you looked at it from the double-door front entrance of the school. There were built-in trophy cases on the wall to the left and a couple of utility closets on the wall to the right. Directly across from the entrance, on the other side of the lobby, was the school office. There was a hallway in front of the office that ran the entire width of the school and housed lockers, class-rooms, and stairs that led to the second floor. A couple of square pillars aesthetically separated the lobby from that hallway.

The prayer circle that day included all eight students who would be shot. Mandy and I were in the corner to the right of the entrance. She was holding my right hand. Kelly was holding my left hand. Kayce was holding Kelly's left hand. Michael would arrive with his guns and stand in front of the trophy cases, across the lobby from where we were and outside of the prayer circle, while we prayed. We joined hands, bowed our heads and closed our eyes. I didn't have a prayer request that day, but prayed intently for those who did. We got through them all and the leader that day, senior Ben Strong, concluded it with a prayer.

"Amen," we all said as we released hands and opened our eyes.

It was time to go to class. I casually walked to my right toward one of the pillars where I had left my Nike book bag. Mandy walked right behind me. It wasn't more than a few steps and a few seconds from the time we left the circle to the time I got to my bag that I heard the horrifying first shot: "POP!" It rang in my ears. I spun around toward the trophy cases, the direction from which the shot came, and I saw Nicole drop hard to the floor. She was near the center of the lobby. It looked like she'd been shot in the head, but I didn't believe it. No way. Though I was looking in his direction, I didn't see Michael with the gun, so when I saw Nicole hit the ground, I was certain this wasn't real. She was just lying there. I saw what looked like blood. I heard the pop. But I really thought she was faking this. It had to be some kind of prank.

I'd never heard a real gun before, other than what was on TV, but that's not at all what this sounded like. This sound was more like firecrackers on the Fourth of July. I figured someone must have put firecrackers nearby where nobody would see them – maybe behind one of the pillars – and Nicole fell as they went off. It certainly seemed more logical than someone firing a gun in our school.

But then, in a matter of a few seconds, came two more slow shots: "POP!" … "POP!" Michael then released a random spray of seven more bullets. It was one of those seven bullets that hit me.

The moment I was shot, my entire body went numb. I crashed to the floor, though having been instantly paralyzed, it felt more like I gently floated down. I never felt the impact with the ground. A girl who had been standing behind me later told me that my legs just gave out. I was lying on my back with my knees bent, pointing to the left toward the lobby doors. I could look straight up and to my right, but that was it. What was strange was I didn't feel any pain. I wasn't crying at all. I still hadn't seen Michael with the gun, so I was unaware that I'd been shot. I honestly didn't know why I was on the ground. All I knew was that I was conscious and couldn't feel anything.

Meanwhile, most of the students who weren't wounded were screaming as they raced down the hallway, all the way to the end and outside a set of doors to the gym. About a half-dozen teachers were either already in the lobby or heading there to help. A few brave students also stayed with us. One of them was Mandy.

I didn't find this out until later, but as the bullets were flying, Mandy felt something go through her hair near the back of her neck. One of my other sisters, Christie, looked at Mandy's neck later at the hospital and found about an inch-long red scrape – a mark left by a bullet, they presumed. That's how close Michael came to probably ending her life. It's amazing to me to think about how Mandy and I came into this world together and came that close to leaving it together. An inch this way or that way for both of us and we'd have been the fourth and fifth fatalities. But it wasn't our time to go. Not yet.

Mandy immediately dropped to the ground when she felt the blast through her hair. Seeing me already down just a few feet from her, she quickly crawled on her hands and knees and hovered over me. She didn't know I'd been shot or why I was down. She just instinctively became my shield. It was ironic because up to that point in our lives, I was usually the one who took care of her. From that moment forward, those roles reversed.

I asked Mandy what was going on. I could tell she was looking intently at something in the direction of the trophy case, but I couldn't lift my head to see what she was looking at. It took me four or five times to ask before she responded.

"There's a gun," she said with panic in her voice.

"There's a gun? Who's got a gun?" I asked her. Again, I had to ask several times.

"Michael," she said quickly.

I knew more than one Michael.

"Michael? Michael who?" I asked her.

"Michael Carneal," she said.

What? Michael Carneal? That didn't make any sense.

Why would he do something like that? Why would he shoot at any of us? As Mandy and I were trying to sort out what was going on, it began to register with us that I must have been shot – but where? There was no blood. No pain. I told Mandy that I couldn't feel my stomach, but neither of us knew what that meant. Had I been shot in the stomach, she certainly would have seen blood, or at least a hole in my shirt. We were both baffled.

Still hovering over me, Mandy was now in a panic. She turned around and saw Kelly standing nearby, holding her left shoulder and looking distraught. Kelly said it hurt and felt like someone had hit her. That's because she, too, had been shot. One of Michael's bullets had grazed her on the back of her shoulder.

Mandy screamed at Mr. Bill Bond, our principal, to do something. Mr. Bond had been in his office on the phone with a parent and had rushed out after hearing all the pandemonium. He cautiously walked toward Michael and positioned himself behind one of the pillars near Michael. He was ready to jump out and try to take the gun away when Michael, suddenly realizing the damage he'd done, thankfully put the gun down. Mr. Bond then grabbed the gun with his right hand, gripped Michael's arm with his left hand, and whisked him into the office without further incident. As excruciating as it was that three girls died, we were so fortunate that there weren't dozens of dead bodies in that lobby, because Michael had the guns and the ammunition to do it.

After Michael was gone, Mandy looked at me with fear.

"Be strong and do not die," she told me sternly. And she left to go to the gym. Mandy was afraid to admit it for the longest time, but she left me because she was simply overwhelmed. Her sister was on the floor paralyzed, she saw Nicole get shot, Kelly had been shot, Mandy was nearly shot herself, and she saw Kayce nearby lying face down, not moving.

Mandy later described her emotional trauma as being "like a two year old wandering around without a mother." Who could blame her for how she felt? She was a 15-year-old girl in the middle of one of the most horrendous events in our country's history. Yes, the shooting was over, but the horror and pain were not.

One of the administrators had already called 911. Most students were now in the gym. Within seconds after Mandy left and with the lobby seeming eerily quiet, Mrs. Dianne Beckman had arrived and knelt by my side. She was my algebra teacher and also taught AP calculus. This was her third year at Heath. She was in her classroom, about three doors down the hallway, preparing for first period when she heard the shots. Like me, she thought the noise was firecrackers, but she soon found out otherwise.

As she pushed her way against the wave of students in the hallway to reach the lobby, she came upon Kayce first, who was lying just a few feet away from me on the other side of the pillar. With two teachers already trying to help Kayce, I was the next one she spotted. Mandy had just left and nobody was tending to me, so Mrs. Beckman knelt down and comforted me while trying to keep me awake. Unable to do any more than that since I wasn't bleeding or in any pain, she closed her eyes and began to pray out loud. She prayed for me, the other wounded students, and for the medical teams to quickly arrive. I quietly gazed at her and listened. Then I interrupted her.

"Am I going to die?" I asked.

"No, you're not going to die. You're going to be fine," she said.

"But I'm paralyzed. I can't feel anything," I said.

"No, you're not paralyzed, you're just in shock," she said adamantly. "You're not paralyzed."

"But I know I am because I can't feel my legs or stomach," I said.

We both knew the truth. We still didn't know where I had been shot, but obviously it had done some serious damage.

Mrs. Beckman remained with me for a few minutes, during which time I started to feel sick and had to throw up. She was very afraid to touch me because I couldn't feel anything and she didn't want to do more damage but, keeping my back and neck stable, she gently and bravely turned me on my side so that I could throw up without choking.

Despite all that had happened to this point, it had only been a minute or two at the most since the shooting. Michael was secured in a conference room in the office. The paramedics were on their way as teachers continued to work together to try to save lives. But now someone else was having difficulty: Jessica.

She had been shot, but nobody, including her, seemed to initially know it. She told Kelly she thought she might have been hit because her body felt funny, but she wasn't sure. In fact, some people later said that Jessica, not knowing that she had a bullet lodged inside her body, actually tried to help some of the others who had been shot. The first time I noticed her she was standing near my feet and complaining that she suddenly felt sick. People around her told her to sit down...then lay down...then she began convulsing. She'd gone from appearing fine and helping others to fighting for her own life in a matter of seconds.

Mrs. Beckman left me and scurried over to her as Jessica rolled around on the ground. I laid there and watched, completely stunned, unable to do anything to help. I couldn't even cry for her, probably because I was in shock. It seemed like there was nothing anybody could do. The bullet had hit one of her main arteries and she was bleeding internally. Coach Tommy Fletcher, my chemistry teacher, held her close. Mrs. Beckman was crying, fearing that Jessica wasn't going to make it.

Sadly, she was right. Jessica died in surgery later that morning.

Mrs. Mary Camille Dummer, a science teacher, had now arrived at my side while Mrs. Beckman was tending to Jessica. Mrs. Dummer had been down the hall in the stairwell when she heard the shots. What's odd, though, is I don't remember her ever being there with me. In fact, it wasn't until nine years later that she and Mrs. Beckman told me that Mrs. Dummer was there, steadfastly holding my hand until the paramedics arrived. I figured I must have been passed out when she was there, but she insists I had my eyes open the entire time and was delirious. Whatever the case, I know I mentally left the lobby and was immersed in a strange dream.

I was dreaming that I was with someone. I don't know who it was or what we were talking about, but we were both walking and laughing. This may sound silly, but I remember someone else riding a bike right at us as we walked, forcing me to quickly jump out of the way to avoid being hit. I didn't know at the time what it all meant, but it felt so real. I wasn't even thinking about the shooting. But then, still walking and laughing with this person, everything suddenly went black and I came back to reality. The first thing I remember was staring up at the lobby ceiling.

"*This* is real," I thought to myself incredulously. "I've really been shot."

Almost a decade later, I read a book entitled *The Dreamer's Dictionary*, written by Lady Stearn Robinson and Tom Corbett.[7] I looked up the word "laughter," something I was doing in the dream with that other person. It said: "If you were laughing in your dream, it signifies approaching unhappiness…" and "if you heard others laughing, it portends a broken friendship."[8] That broken friendship could have referred to Michael and me. It also could have referred to Kayce and me. She was my friend who was dying just a few feet away from me.

Another word I looked up in that dictionary was "walk," which I was also doing in the dream. It said that a dream involving walking was a form of "obstacle dream." It said that if you walk with difficulty, as I did when the bike nearly ran me over, "you will still overcome your obstacles, but it will require determined effort."[9] That would prove to be very profound as I battled back from what happened to me that day. After nearly a decade, that bizarre dream finally seemed to have some meaning.

Despite the chaos, devastation, and my condition, I had a sense of calm after I came out of the dream; I was going to be OK. I think almost immediately after the shooting I felt like I might die, but after the dream I felt everything was going to be fine. There were no tears; no fear of death; not even a worry anymore about the lack of feeling I had in my stomach or legs. Maybe shock played a part in that. Maybe it was something about the dream that I can't remember that put me at peace. I don't know. I just know at that moment, I wasn't afraid of anything.

The ambulances finally arrived. I have no idea how long they took to get there. Some people said 30 minutes. Others said 15 minutes. Some said less than 10 minutes. Mr. Bond said it was 13 minutes. It's interesting how in a situation like that, time can fly by for some and stand still for others. I know for me it felt like an eternity, but that's probably not surprising given the condition I was in. Having to go through morning rush-hour traffic and then travel the narrow, two-lane country roads to get to Heath, I know the paramedics got there as quickly as they could, and they worked diligently as soon as they arrived. They immediately went to those who needed help first: Nicole, Kayce, and Jessica. I asked the paramedics as they walked by me when it would be my turn. They told me after those three, they would get me.

As I lay there watching the others being taken out on gurneys, I still felt like I was going to be OK. I knew I was paralyzed, but I was also convinced that I was going to live. I couldn't help, though, but think of those who were in worse shape than I was. Were they going to die?

Was there anybody else hurt whom I didn't know about? Where was Mandy? Was she OK? Did my parents know what happened? And what about Michael?

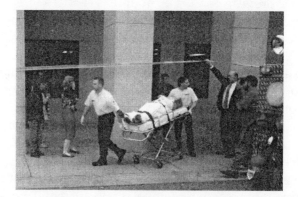

This is the scene from outside the school after the shooting.
(December 2, 1997, *Paducah Sun*/
Barkley Thieleman)

Did he really do this? If so, why? What was his motive? Where did he get a gun? Why us? Why anybody?

These questions racing through my mind were interrupted by the paramedics, who were ready for me now. They gently slid me on a board, onto a gurney, and quickly wheeled me out the front doors of the school. I was rushed to Lourdes Hospital about ten miles away. What was supposed to be a regular Monday for me and everybody else at Heath turned out to be one of the deadliest school shootings in history. Two hours earlier I was lying comfortably and safely in my own bed. Now I was lying in the back of an ambulance with no feeling below my chest and no clue of what I was about to face.

Just 23 days short of my 16th birthday, my life had changed forever.

2

Just Two Ordinary Kids

Michael and I weren't the closest friends growing up since we were in different grades, but when we talked or were around each other, we got along well. We had some things in common: we were both in band, shared some of the same friends, lived within a few blocks of each other, and attended the same middle and high schools.

Of course, we were also very different in many ways.

I was born December 24, 1981, at Western Baptist Hospital in Paducah. It was a Cesarean birth with Mandy born two minutes before me. Mom named Mandy, but Mom's sister, Ann Brewer (whom we call "Sissy"), named me since she never had a daughter. Sissy chose "Melissa Joyce" simply because she always liked the name "Melissa." The middle name is after my mom.

We were the fifth and sixth (and last) children of Ray and Joyce Jenkins, born 21 years after their eldest child. My brother Mike was born in 1960, followed by Pam in 1962, and Susie in 1967. Christie was born in 1973, nearly nine years before Mandy and me. Despite the age differences, we were always a very close family.

Mandy (left) and me

I always looked at Christie as a second mom – and my hero. She watched us when Mom and Dad went out, read us stories, and played with us constantly. When she had friends over, we bugged her continuously. She had every reason to get aggravated and cast us away, but she never did.

Christie had been a student at the University of Kentucky but transferred to Paducah Community College in the fall of 1997 to help take care of my mom. Mom began having health problems that fall, which confined her to a wheelchair most of the time. After the shooting, with Mom and me both in wheelchairs, Christie graciously postponed her education indefinitely and selflessly dedicated the next two years of her life to taking care of us. Despite the lack of a college degree, she's gone on to have a successful career in the insurance industry in Nashville, Tennessee. I always felt Christie could do absolutely everything, and that's exactly how I wanted to be.

I was also close to my brother and other sisters, even though they were so much older. Susie was in high school when we were born and was also like a mother to us, though I don't remember much since we were so young when she lived at home. My earliest recollection of her is when she got married. Mandy and I were about four years old and didn't get to go to the wedding, but we were so excited because we thought she was getting married where she worked: ShowBiz Pizza! We were disappointed to find out the ceremony was actually at the courthouse, but it was still fun to throw rice in her face when she came home after the wedding. She is married, has one child, and lives in West Paducah.

Mike and Pam had already moved out of the house by the time we were born, but we grew up also knowing them. Like the rest of the family, they were there for me after the shooting, helping any way they could at the hospital or home. Both are married and live in West Paducah. Mike and his wife have two children. Pam and her husband have one child. In fact, Pam's son, Winston, is just a week younger than Mandy and me. We grew up with him and attended Heath middle and high schools together. He was there the day of the shooting. Fortunately, he was in his biology classroom upstairs when it happened and was unharmed, but he told me later that he saw me from that classroom window being wheeled out of school and into an ambulance. He's one of many students that day who suffered no physical injuries but was left with a heavy emotional burden.

Our hometown of West Paducah is in McCracken County and has a population of between 25,000 to 30,000 people.[10] It's part of the Bible belt and rests on the Ohio River, just south of Metropolis, Illinois (Superman's hometown), about an hour east of Missouri, and an hour north of Tennessee. As in many farm communities today, developers are buying up land and building homes. It's steadily growing with pockets of it becoming more modernized with many chain stores and restaurants. But before the shooting, the average person probably never heard of Paducah. The town's biggest claim to fame was (and probably still is) the American Quilter's Society Museum, which attracts quilting fanatics from around the world every spring.

Like most everyone I knew there, we were a pretty typical middle-class family. Mom stayed home to raise us. Dad worked at Paducah Power System and occasionally on the side as an electrician. He retired the summer before the shooting because of some health problems, but now works at a local department store to keep busy. They were fun parents, taking us on family vacations and involving themselves in our activities. Even when we were bad, they had a sense of humor. For

example, if Mandy and I fought, Mom would sometimes make us sit down in front of the television tuned
to the country music station. We hated country music
and would act as if our worlds were ending when she
did that. But they were also strict parents, giving us
chores and raising us to be responsible. Mandy was
usually better behaved. I was the mischievous one,
seeing what I could get away with – such as setting our
bathroom on fire, swinging an axe to a can of paint, and
breaking curfew.

We were about five years old when the fire happened.
Mandy and I were too scared to go to the bathroom
alone, so we always went together. One day Mandy was
sitting on the toilet while I was impatiently waiting for
her to finish. Looking for something to do to pass the
time, I reached up on the bathroom counter and took
one of Mom's hair picks. Intrigued by this pick, I decided
to see what would happen if I stuck it in the wall heater.

Bad idea.

The pick caught fire. I dropped it on the floor in a
panic, igniting our 1970s shag carpet. I ran out screaming
for Mom who was on the phone in another room. Mandy,
whom I left sitting on the toilet, leapt off it with her
pants around her ankles and ran out because she didn't
like to be in the bathroom alone – and probably because
I started a fire in there. Mom raced in and, wearing
nothing on her feet but nylons, stomped it out. Mandy
and I stared at her in awe as if she were some kind of
superhero.

I continued to turn my parents' hair grayer as I got
older. In sixth grade Mandy, Taylor, and I took a stroll
into the woods near our house. The boys in the neighborhood had a clubhouse there made of plywood that
was nailed to a couple trees, and we decided we were
going to mess it up. I had taken Dad's pickaxe from his
shed. Yeah, we were serious. When we got to the clubhouse, I noticed some cans of black spray paint lying

around that belonged to the boys. I said to my partners in crime, "You know what? I'm going to mess those cans up, too!" I swung the pickaxe down as hard as I could. Now I'm not sure what I thought was going to happen when I broke one open, but for some reason, it never occurred to me that we'd end up looking like three Dalmatians, speckled from head to toe in black paint. But we did. It was something we obviously couldn't hide from our parents. To nobody's surprise, we were grounded.

The worst and last bad thing I did was in 1996, the summer before my freshman year. I met a cute boy at band camp who was a junior and could drive – very cool to a teen like me who was still too young to be behind the wheel. One night we played miniature golf where he worked. I was supposed to go home right after the course closed at nine o'clock, but he had to stay late to clean up. So I waited...and waited...and waited. By the time he was finished, it was well past my curfew, so we cruised around for a while. I figured I was already late, so what was the harm in being later? When I got home about eleven o'clock, I found out what the harm was. My parents were in such a panic that Dad was out searching for me. Mom was furious.

"I'm never going to trust you again," she said in a calm, but stern voice. "Go to your room."

I did. And I laid there in bed in a lot of pain – mental pain. She didn't physically hurt me. She didn't ground me. She simply said she couldn't trust me. That stung more than anything else she could have done. I learned my lesson. That night was the last time I ever did anything like that, and I was fortunate enough to regain her trust as the years went on.

Despite the stunts I pulled outside of school, I was always well-behaved in school and a pretty good student. I earned mostly As and Bs at Concord Elementary and Heath Middle schools, with an occasional C in high school. I didn't like math but loved science. I played soccer in middle school and the flute in band starting in sixth grade.

Socially, I was into pop rock music with New Kids on the Block being my favorite. I had a ton of friends in our neighborhood, and we were never bored. We were into sports, lemonade stands, Barbies, and exploring in the woods. There was always something to do.

Physically, I was pretty overweight throughout elementary school and early in middle school. In sixth grade Mom let me get a perm. Picture a heavy, brown-haired girl with a perm and glasses. But I started to blossom in seventh grade. I got highlights in my hair and really focused on getting healthy by exercising and eating right. I went from about a size 16 to a size 5. In eighth grade I got contacts and bleached my hair blonde. It's a look I've pretty much stuck with.

Spiritually, I have always believed in God. Mom told us Bible stories and I prayed often as a child. It wasn't until sixth grade, however, that I started going to church. Until then, Mom had to take care of my grandpa all the time and church was not a priority. After Grandpa died, we went every week to 32nd Street Church of Christ.

Mandy and I loved going to church so much that we chose to be baptized in February 1996 when we were in eighth grade. What an experience! It was a Sunday night after the regular church service in front of a pretty large crowd. We had to take off all our clothes, put on robes, and stand in a warm tub of water. At first it was a bit scary. They placed a cloth over my nose, dipped me backward, fully submerged me, and then pulled me up. It was an amazing feeling, though, when it was finished – one of absolute happiness. There was no doubt in my mind when it was over that it was the right thing to do. I think it was good timing, too, given that I was about to embark on a new phase in my life in about six months that would include new challenges and pressures: high school.

We were difficult to tell apart, even as teens. I'm on the left.

My freshman year at Heath was fun, and I adjusted pretty easily. Since Heath Middle School is the only middle school to feed into the high school, I knew most of the freshmen going in. And being from such a close community, I knew a lot of the older students, too. The only extracurricular activity I participated in my freshman year was playing flute in the band, but I had much bigger and more exciting plans my remaining three years there.

My sophomore year I was elected president of Future Homemakers of America (FHA), now known as Family, Career & Community Leaders of America (FCCLA). I was looking forward to being part of Kaleidoscope that year, a class in which I would sing and dance in a choir production. My plan was to play soccer my junior year and continue in the band.

But Michael ripped all of that away from me in a matter of seconds.

I was just becoming active in my FHA presidency when the shooting forced me to relinquish that office. I would join Kaleidoscope, but participating in a class that involved dancing wasn't the same in a wheelchair. Obviously soccer was no longer an option for me, either. I continued to play the flute in the marching band, minus the marching. I had to sit isolated on the sidelines and play while the rest of my band mates marched on the field. Everything that I'd worked for and strived for was suddenly gone.

What Michael did to us that day still doesn't make sense. No matter how many different answers I get from court depositions, psychological evaluations, people who knew him, or Michael himself, I don't think I'll ever fully understand it. That's because I'll never be able to forget the Michael I knew before this happened.

Michael, believe it or not, was nice, funny, and generally pretty cool to hang around. In fact, when we had band competitions that required road trips those first few months of my sophomore year, I made sure to be on his bus and sit near him. He was so outgoing and funny. He kept us laughing on those long rides, making time fleeting. I, on the other hand, was a very shy person who could never act silly in front of other people like he did. I admired him for being like that and wished I could be that outgoing.

We went to the middle school together but really didn't know each other until high school. I came to know him mainly through Taylor and another friend we had in common, Eric Frazier. Michael and I were in band together my sophomore year, which was his freshman year. I played the flute. I think he played the baritone. He was a somewhat small kid, just over five feet tall and maybe 125 pounds. Some kids thought he was kind of nerdy, but I never thought that because he was always so nice.

His dad was a respected attorney in town. His mom was a homemaker who always seemed to be involved in school, usually with the band. Kelly Carneal, his sister, was also in the band and a senior that year. I didn't know her well, but she always seemed friendly. She was very bright and was valedictorian of her class.

The family belonged to St. Paul Lutheran Church in West Paducah. There initially were media reports that Michael was an atheist. I know that wasn't true. His minister, the Rev. Paul Donner, came to Michael's defense after the shooting to dispel those rumors. He'd known the Carneals for three decades and baptized Michael as a baby. He had confirmed Michael in the spring of 1997 after two years of confirmation classes.[11]

Taylor could also vouch for his Christianity. She used to attend church camps with him.

There were also reports that he was aiming for members of our prayer group when he opened fire. I never believed that, at least not in the sense that he was aiming at us because of our belief in God. Mr. Bond believes he was aiming for us because our group contained many of the brightest kids in the school. Kelly Hard believes he was aiming for us because he knew we wouldn't fight back. It is my feeling he just figured that the lobby would be the most crowded place in the school at that time, so that was the place to carry out the shooting. I don't think it mattered to him whether it was us or another group.

I can't say there was a whole lot out of the ordinary about him. He typically dressed in jeans and a tee shirt. Some of the kids he hung out with dressed differently, gothic-like, if you will, but that was never odd to me. Some of those same kids were my friends, too. Michael was always joking around, the "class clown" of the band.

One day at band camp in the summer of 1997 he wore a button he made that had pictures of Mandy and me on it. He ran around during one of our breaks showing it to everybody and saying we were fat. We chased him around, trying to take it from him, but all in fun. We eventually got it, took it home that night, and replaced our pictures with a doctored photo of him. He laughed when he saw it the next day. He always appeared to be able to take it as well as he could dish it out.

Some of the older band kids picked on Michael a lot, but if it bothered him, he never let on. Many of them told him to shut up after he'd do or say something silly, but just as many laughed at his antics because they thought he was funny. I rarely saw him be serious about anything but, as I said earlier, that was something I really liked about him. In fact, one of the only times I can

remember him being serious was the last time I was
around him about ten days before the shooting when
we'd both attended a classmate's birthday party at her
house. Michael and I didn't talk much that night, and he
didn't seem to be in his usual joking mood.

After having cake and opening gifts, some of the
chaperones took us to the riverfront to walk around,
look at shops, and listen to a band. After that we went to
the shore of the river. When it was time to leave, most of
the kids climbed some rocks to get back up the road.
Being uncomfortable doing that, a male friend and I
decided to walk along the river to the boat ramp that
would take us up to the road. Michael saw us walking in
that direction and yelled, "Go get you some," as if we
were going off on our own with other things in mind.
My reaction to Michael was the same as always: I laughed
it off. It didn't offend me. It's just who he was, always a
clown.

When Michael was questioned by detectives after
the shooting, he said he was mad because everybody
made fun of him. Yes, he was teased and bullied by
some kids, but the irony is that he made fun of people all
the time to get a laugh. Maybe that was his defense
against the treatment he had to endure. Maybe it truly
did hurt him and he kept those feelings bottled up until
that fateful day.

He never appeared to me to be mentally ill or insane
(as he would later claim he was), but whatever his issues
were, I can think of a thousand better ways that he could
have handled his problems than the way he did. There
was no excuse good enough to justify leaving three
innocent kids dead and five wounded.

We can all look back and say the shooting could
have been avoided if someone would have said this or
done that, but the bottom line is that it was solely his
decision. And it wasn't a spur-of-the-moment thing. As
he made clear when he was interrogated by a detective

just hours after the shooting, he thought it through and went to extreme measures to make it happen.

Sadly, the only part he didn't consider in his plan was the death and devastation he would leave behind.

3

WHY?

Michael has been interrogated several times over the years by law enforcement officials, attorneys, psychiatrists, and psychologists about why he did what he did. But I think one of the most interesting interviews, and certainly the most timely, was conducted by Detective Carl Baker of the McCracken County Sheriff's Department at 9:42 A.M. on December 1, 1997, just two hours after the shooting. It took place in a tiny room at the sheriff's department and was recorded on audio and video tape. The room was barely big enough for the three chairs and rectangular table that were in it. Michael and his attorney, Chuck Granner, sat on one side. Detective Baker sat on the other side.

Michael was pretty fidgety throughout, tugging at the long sleeves of his shirt and often putting his hand over his mouth, I assume out of nervousness. He answered all the questions Detective Baker threw at him, mostly in a calm and matter-of-fact way, though he did cry at times. He explained how he went to great lengths to obtain the guns, ammunition, and sneak it all into the school that morning. It appears he thought of everything except the consequences of his actions. In the transcript, "CB" is Baker, "MC" is Michael and "CG" is Granner.

CB: Needless to say, there's, there's been something that's happened and that's why we were called. You do understand that? You do understand that I'm not going to tell you any details 'cause a lot of those details I don't know, but there are some people hurt, OK?

MC: Uh-huh (Yes).

CB: My question to you, my main question is to you is – what I would like for you to do is to start – well let's just start this morning, was about what time you got up, what was on your mind, what were you thinking and what you did all the way through up until the officers put you with the guidance counselor.

MC: OK, well, it was about 6:45.

CB: That what time you got up?

MC: Yes, and I got up and took a shower like normally and then I got back in my room and it was about seven and I put on my clothes and then I, um, um, had this bundle of guns and it, they were wrapped up in a blanket.

CB: What, do you know what kind of guns they were?

MC: There were two shot guns and two .22s. And then uh, took 'em and, uh, went over there and then I went to the garage and sat it by my sister's car.

CB: You what? Wait a minute – you did what now? You took 'em out of the house?

MC: Yeah, I just walked through the house and set 'em by my sister's car.

CB: Was anybody up when you was walking through the house?

MC: Uh, yeah, my mom.

CB: Did she ask you what was in the bundle?

MC: Uh-uh (No).

CB: Did she see it?

MC: Uh-uh.

CB: OK.

MC: And then I went back into my room and filled my backpack up with shotgun shells.

CB: What color's the backpack?

MC: Olive.

CB: OK.

MC: And then I put some .22 bullets in a box and put 'em in there and, um, walked out and it was about 7:17 'cause I looked at the clock and everybody's like you better leave so my sister and me walked out to the car and she asked me what was in the bundle and I told her, I told her it was some stuff for an English project and then she asked what was in it and I just told her it was some, um, props for a play and I took 'em and I put 'em in the trunk with my backpack and she drove to school and I got out in the parking lot and I carried it and, um, I walked into the lobby area and I sat it down on the side there by my backpack.

CB: OK, when you went in the, do you know about what time it was when you got to school?

MC: Um, 7:25 I think.

CB: Did you look at a clock or...

MC: Yeah, they got 'em all up along the walls.

CB: OK, so it was about 7:25 when you got into school?

MC: Yeah.

CB: And when you went through this, there's an outside set of double doors, then the inside set of double doors.

MC: Yes.

CB: Which direction did you go when you went through the double doors?

MC: Well, I came in and here's the school parking lot, we parked at the back.

CB: OK.

MC: And I walked through behind the school building and into the band room and I walked through the band room and I walked down through the auditorium and then there's a part where they started building on the high school from the auditorium and I walked up there and passed the office and into the lobby.

CB: So you was in the band room and in the auditorium?

MC: Yes.

CB: And then you walked up towards the office?

MC: Yeah.

CB: OK, where'd you set your backpack down at?

MC: Up against these glass cabinets in the lobby, they've got trophies in 'em.

CB: OK, standing at the double doors looking at the office.

MC: Yeah, they're on the left.

CB: On the – against the wall over there?

MC: Yeah.

CB: And that's where you laid the blanket and your backpack.

MC: Uh-huh.

CB: And what was going through your mind at the time?

MC: Um, everybody was asking me what was in it and I kept telling them props for an English skit and I just really didn't know what I was gonna do.

CB: OK, when did you, when did you first decide to take the guns to the school?

MC: Um, Thursday.

CB: And why?

MC: I, I don't know.

CB: Was you mad at somebody?

MC: Not anybody in particular.

CB: Several people? Your Mom and Dad?

MC: Uh-uh.

CB: Wasn't mad at your mom and dad?

MC: Uh-uh.

CB: Mad at the teachers?

MC: Not really.
CB: Had you gotten a bad grade on anything?
MC: Uh-uh.
CB: You mad at the principal?
MC: Uh-uh. I guess I just got mad 'cause everybody kept making fun of me.
CB: Why were they making fun?
MC: For all kinds of things.
CB: Calling you names and that kind of stuff?
MC: Uh-huh.
CB: How long have you been going to, to that school?
MC: The high – to Heath?
CB: Yes.
MC: Since third grade.
CB: OK, so you had some pretty good friends there?
MC: Couple, couple.
CB: Couple, OK. Did you talk to them about it?
MC: Uh-uh.
CB: Nobody knew what was going on except for you?
MC: Uh-uh. Unless, well, well see like at the lunch table we talk about stuff and I, and, I don't know, I guess we started talking about bringing a gun to school or something and taking over and I guess.
CB: OK, you said we, who's we?
MC: Like me and Toby Nace and we would always eat together.
CB: Just you and him?
MC: Yeah, other people would come around sometimes but they were always different people.
CB: But he was the one you talked to about it the most?
MC: Yeah.
CB: What, what kinda things, you said they were making fun of you, what kind of things were they calling you, what kind of names were they calling?
MC: Um, nerd and they were always calling me crack baby and freak.
CB: Why would they call you crack baby, don't know?

(At this point, Michael begins to cry)

MC: 'Cause I'm different I guess. My mom always said that they were just jealous because I got better grades but I knew it wasn't true.

CB: Well, if you made good grades you done a lot better than I did. I didn't make good grades in school. Anybody in particular that made you mad?

MC: Uh-uh.

CB: Was there any one person that done more of this than anybody else?

MC: Gary Abernatha.

CB: Was this like an everyday thing?

MC: Yeah, like sometimes, in ICP, which is Science, I would say something like telling him to be quiet or something 'cause he was always making fun of me, when we got out of the class he would hit me, just like right in the head for no reason.

(Michael cries some more)

CB: Why would he do that? Did he ever tell you why he did it? Hit you with his fist? Was it always his fist or did he use something else?

MC: Sometimes he would kick me in the shin.

CB: Did you tell teachers?

MC: Uh, they don't do much.

CB: Did you ever tell the principal? But he wasn't the only one?

MC: No.

CB: But he was the main one? OK, did you spend the night with somebody Saturday night?

MC: Um, they spent the night at my house.

CB: OK, and who was that?

MC: Michael Alonso.

CB: Alonso?

MC: Yeah, A-L-O-N-S-O.

CB: Did ya'll talk about it?

MC: Uh-uh.

CB: What did you talk to him about?

MC: Nothing, we mainly just watched TV and played PlayStation.

CB: Did you give him some stuff to hang onto for you?

MC: Yeah.

CB: What kind of stuff did you give him?

MC: A gun.

CB: What kind of gun?

MC: It was a rifle, a 30-30.

CB: Why'd you give him the gun?

MC: Because, well there's a .22 also.

CB: Pistol or rifle?

MC: Rifle. And another .22 rifle.

CB: You give him three guns?

MC: Yeah, well see, I took 'em over there and, uh, and I didn't have any way to get 'em home.

CB: But that's not the guns that you took to school this morning?

MC: No.

CB: And he's still got 'em far as you know?

MC: Yeah.

CB: OK, uh, take just a second, I'll be right back.
    (Baker leaves the room)

CG: Anything you need, Michael?

MC: Uh-uh.

CG: You OK?

MC: Yeah.

CG: What's the name of the boy that picked on you a lot?

MC: Gary Abernatha.
    (Baker re-enters the room)

CB: Chuck?

CG: Yes, sir.

CB: Come here just a second, please.

CG: Sure.
    (Baker and Granner leave the room for a minute, then both come back, finishing their conversation as they re-enter the room)

CB: Try to save a little face here.

CG: Right.

CB: For everybody. OK, so I guess what I need you to do now is, is just, you went in to school.

MC: Uh-huh.

CB: You put the blanket down.

MC: Uh-huh

CB: And you put your backpack down.

MC: Uh-huh.

CB: Beside the, the glass cabinets.

MC: Uh-huh.

CB: And what was the next thing that you did. Well let me do just one better than that. What was going on?

MC: Well, everybody was just around talking.

CB: That early in the morning?

MC: Yeah, the, then I was just, like, standing there and then my friend Toby came up and we started talking and then everybody was just like "Time to pray," and everybody got in this big circle and started praying.

CB: What'd you and Toby talk about?

MC: Nothing really, we just...

CB: Did you tell him what was in the, in the blanket?

MC: Uh-uh.

CB: He didn't, he didn't know either?

MC: Uh-uh.

CB: OK, OK, they was all in a circle.

MC: Yeah.

CB: And somebody said, "Let's pray."

MC: Yeah, they said, "Let's pray," and everybody got in this big circle and started praying.

CB: OK.

MC: And then I was just sitting there and I reached in my backpack and pulled out a handgun.

CB: What kind of handgun was it?

MC: It was a .22 Ruger, and I put in a clip and turned off the safety and cocked it and then just started firing.

CB: Who all was standing in that group, do you know?

MC: Uh-uh.

CB: Did, did you know any of the kids in that group?

MC: I knew Ben.

CB: Ben? Ben who?

MC: I don't know his last name, he's on the football team.

CB: OK. Uh, uh, white guy? African-American?

MC: He's white.

CB: OK, how old is he, do you know?

MC: He's a senior.

CB: So that'd put him at least 17 or 18, right?

MC: Yeah, and then, and then I stopped and I realized what was going on and I just sat down and Ben popped up from behind a column and told me to calm down. So I set the gun down and he, he came over there and he, he was telling to me to calm down and not worry about it.

CB: That was Ben?

MC: Yeah.

CB: Is he kinda, sort of a friend or just somebody you know?

MC: He's nice to me.

CB: OK.

MC: And then Mr. Bond came out there and grabbed me and jerked me away and we, and then he pulled me down the hall and Ben kept yelling, "I need to talk to him for a minute." Mr. Bond just said, "Get away," and Ben had to turn around and go back.

CB: Yeah. But Ben, Ben was wanting to, he was wanting to listen to you.

MC: Uh-huh.

CB: Listen to what you had to say?

MC: Uh-huh.

CB: So, so you liked Ben a lot?

MC: Uh-huh.

CB: So he, he wasn't one that was shot then right?

MC: Uh-uh.

CB: OK, did, do you know anybody's names specific

who, who you might have hit?

MC: Uh-uh.

CB: Do you know how many rounds you fired?

MC: I think maybe, um, eight – either eight or ten.

CB: Eight or ten?

MC: Yeah.

CB: Was there anybody in that group, specific, that you was angry with?

MC: Uh-uh.

CB: Was, um, Mr. Abernatha in that group?

MC: Uh-uh.

CB: He wasn't?

MC: Uh-uh.

CB: I know this is – I know it's difficult, believe me, it is difficult. It's difficult for me 'cause I have kids, uh, I have one your age, uh, and I know how I would feel – I'd be like your father. I'd be tore up, uh, you know, but there are, you know, there's things we just have to ask, I know it's difficult.

MC: Uh-huh.

CB: So if you need to take a break, you tell me so, and we'll do that or whatever. Um, about a week ago...

MC: Uh-huh.

CB: Approximately, did you tell anybody else that you was gonna do this or was this when you was talking to Toby about, you all was talking about bringing one and taking over the school or whatever?

MC: Oh, we been talking about, we been talking about it for, for a long time.

CB: How long, month or two months?

MC: About a year.

CB: Really? What, what started the conversation about it?

MC: I don't remember, we just always talked about it and stuff.

CB: Did, did you see it anywhere or read, excuse me, read it or anything like that?

MC: I don't know but there was one movie where a guy walked into some kind of, I don't know, he walked into something with a shotgun and started shooting a lot of people, some kind of movie or something.

CB: You don't know the name of it or anything?

MC: It was, "Basketball Diaries."

CB: "Basketball Diaries?" What went through your mind while you was firing the gun?

MC: I don't know, it was all, like, blurry and foggy, I just didn't know what was going on. I think I closed my eyes for a minute.

CB: Did you just stand right there?

MC: Uh-huh.

CB: Or did you walk?

MC: I just stood there.

CB: You just stood in that one spot?

MC: Uh-huh.

CB: Did anybody else say anything to you other than Ben?

MC: Uh, no. No.

CB: Where was Toby?

MC: I, I don't know, he, he ran off.

CB: He took off? And when Mr. Bond took you in the, I guess in the conference room is what they call it.

MC: Yeah.

CB: Did he say anything to you?

MC: Uh-uh, he just sat me down and then Mr. Dulworth – he's a senior English teacher.

CB: OK.

MC: He sat in there with me.

CB: Was that who was sitting in there with you when I got there?

MC: Yeah.

CB: OK. That's Mr. Dulworth?

MC: Yeah.

CB: Did he say anything to you?

MC: He, he asked me why I did it?

CB: And what'd you tell him?

MC: I told him I didn't know and he asked me if I had been hearing voices or something.

CB: What'd you tell him?

MC: Uh-uh.

CB: Told him you hadn't been hearing any voices or anything?

MC: I hadn't been hearing any.

CB: Is he kinda sorta a guidance counselor or is English all he does?

MC: He, he's an English teacher but everybody likes him, he's really nice.

CB: You like him? Is he, he's nice to you too?

MC: Yeah.

CB: Do you trust him? And I guess shortly thereafter then, the police officer arrived.

MC: Yeah.

CB: OK, and then they advised you of what your rights were?

MC: He, he, I had all my stuff sitting on the table, it was in my pocket.

CB: Yeah, I've got it right here.

MC: And he patted me down and cuffed me and he sat me down in the chair and then about 30 minutes, or 20 minutes later, um, some guy came in and read me my rights.

CB: OK, but nobody, no law enforcement officer, talked to you after that?

MC: Uh-uh.

CB: Until I come in there and explained how we were gonna go out of the building and everything?

MC: Uh-huh.

CB: Uh, let's get back to the guns. The, the 30-30 and the two .22 rifles.

MC: Uh-huh.

CB: That you give to Mr. Alonso.

MC: Uh-huh.

CB: Where did those come from?

MC: I stole 'em.

CB: Where did you steal them from?

MC: Toby's.

CB: Does he know it?

MC: I don't think so.

CB: They belong to his father?

MC: Yes.

CB: You know what his father's name is?

MC: Wendall.

CB: When did you steal them?

MC: Thursday.

CB: This last Thursday?

MC: Yes.

CB: About what time?

MC: Um.

CB: Daytime, nighttime, afternoon?

MC: It was starting to get dark.

CB: About what they call dusk?

MC: Yeah.

CB: OK, did you break in the house?

MC: Uh-uh, they're in this garage they have locked up in this gun cage and I knew where he kept the keys.

CB: Did you take any ammunition?

MC: Yeah, a bunch of shotgun shells.

CB: OK, a bunch, how, boxes or just loose ones or what?

MC: One, two, uh, there's one, two, three, four, five, six, about seven boxes, eight, eight boxes and then, um.

CB: And that was just shotgun shells?

MC: Yeah and then there was four big, big boxes of .22s and then there's two more smaller boxes.

CB: OK, there was four big boxes of .22s?

MC: There was four boxes of 500 and there was two boxes of 550.

CB: And then two boxes of 550?

MC: Yeah.

CB: And that all come from Toby's father.

MC: Yeah.

CB: OK. Um, the guns you had in the blanket, where did they come from? There was two shotguns.

MC: Yeah, they came from that same place.

CB: All of the long guns come from there?

MC: Uh-huh.

CB: Or did all of the guns come from there?

MC: All of them came from there.

CB: Even the .22 pistol?

MC: Uh-huh.

CB: Was Toby with you?

MC: Uh-uh. He didn't know.

CB: How'd you get over there?

MC: Well, I went over there just to hang out 'cause he lives down the street from me and then about, well I don't know it was about three o'clock, I told him I had to leave, he was like OK, and then I rode my bike about half way, then I turned around and rode up behind their shed and climbed in the window.

CB: To the garage?

MC: Yeah, and then I got, I got the key and then I opened up the...

CB: Was the window opened?

MC: It was unlocked.

CB: OK, but you had to open a window?

MC: Yeah.

CB: OK.

MC: And then I, um, got the key and opened up the gun cabinet and took all the guns.

CB: OK.

MC: And then, uh, walked across the garage and there's this little box with a handgun in it and I got the handgun and then I ran out, I climbed out the window and then I, um...

CB: How'd you carry 'em home?

MC: I had a green duffel bag that was in there.

CB: Five, six, seven, and then seven long guns and one pistol?

MC: Yeah, about that.

CB: And you had a big long duffel bag?

MC: Yeah, big Army one.

CB: OK.

MC: And then there's a cow field on the other side, see he lives on this other street and I live down here.

CB: OK.

MC: There's a cow field right here.

CB: OK.

MC: And I walked into the cow field and I went up into the barn and started looking at all the guns and then it was dark by then so I went to my house and set 'em in front of the window, 'cause our windows are way up and then I went into my room and locked the door and climbed out the window and got 'em and hid 'em in the closet.

CB: OK, where's the duffel bag?

MC: It's at Michael Alonso's.

CB: That's what the other guns were in?

MC: Yeah.

CB: OK.

MC: My parents they used to look around at all my stuff and make sure I didn't have anything bad.

CB: Uh-huh.

MC: And then I went to this party and it got real rough so I left and they trusted me.

(Michael begins to cry again)

CB: OK.

MC: And they trusted me and that's when I did it.

CB: So they quit looking in your room?

MC: They, they used to snoop around and everything and I told them I didn't like it and they still did it but then they, when I left the party 'cause it got too rough they started trusting me about stuff.

CB: OK. Did, uh, were, were you mad at your parents about anything?

MC: Uh-uh.

CB: I know I asked you that a little while ago but, sounds like you might be angry with 'em?

MC: Uh-uh, they're, they're really nice to me.

CB: Didn't have any, anything you really wanted that they wouldn't get for you or, I mean you had, you looked like you got good clothes and that kind of stuff. They took care of you pretty good?

MC: Uh-huh.

CB: Did, uh, I think I may have already asked you but I'll ask you again, did Mr. Alonso know what you were doing?

MC: Uh-uh.

CB: Did you ever tell him you was taking any of these guns to school?

MC: Uh-uh.

CB: Toby was the only one that you really talked to about taking guns to school?

MC: Yeah.

CB: Did he know it was this day?

MC: Uh-uh.

CB: Did anybody know it was this day?

MC: Um, no.

CB: Wasn't somebody last week, some time that you told that today was gonna be the day?

MC: No, not unless they, I don't know.

CB: Not unless they what?

MC: I don't know, not unless I was just talking about it, but I don't remember telling anybody. I would remember that.

CB: OK, gimme just one second. I need to check on the tape and make sure it's still – 'cause I forgot to turn that one on, so.

(Baker leaves the room, then comes back after about a minute)

CB: OK, just, just a couple more things – I got just a very little bit of tape left, so I want to make sure I get it in.

MC: All right.

CB: Uh, yeah, I can start that one if I think that one's gonna run out. Just a couple of quick questions.

MC: All right.

CB: The ear plugs that were in your pocket.

MC: Uh-huh.

CB: Where'd they come from?

MC: The, the garage, they were in the gun cabinet.

CB: Oh, so they also came from...

MC: Yeah, the top of the gun cabinet.

CB: OK, now, one very important question – and you can think about it a minute before you answer or, whatever, it's up to you. When you reached in that backpack and pulled the, the, the .22 pistol out, what, what color was it?

MC: Chrome.

CB: OK.

(The cassette tape ends here, but the video tape keeps rolling)

CB: When you pulled the trigger the first time.

MC: Uh-huh.

CB: Did you realize people could get hurt?

MC: I, I don't know, I really wasn't thinking until, until I stopped shooting.

CB: OK, when you took the guns to school had you thought about the fact that somebody was probably gonna get hurt?

MC: No, uh-uh.

CB: You don't know?

MC: I didn't.

CB: Your plan was, I think like you said before, that what you and Toby had been discussing, was to take over, just take over the school?

MC: Yeah, but I, I knew it wouldn't work.

CB: Um, I'm gonna go ahead and tell him what he's gonna be charged with, uh, just so he'll know. First thing is burglary, first degree, that's all the guns.

MC: All right.

CB: Uh, second thing is – I don't know how many counts yet – but there are gonna be several counts of what's called first degree assault.

MC: Uh-huh.

CB: And there's gonna be at least one count of murder.

MC: Uh-huh.

CB: Now that's all I know for sure right now. Uh, do you have anything, Chuck, you need to ask of me because I, like I said, as far as names of people and exactly how many, I, I don't know yet because everything was so shambled out there with parents and stuff.

CG: I have no questions yet, detective. (Granner explains to Baker that Mr. Carneal asked Granner to sit in on the interview and that he has no additional questions at this time).

CG: His parents will ask me where he will go from here.

CB: He will go to detention, um, and he will be held at least until in the morning, until 8:40, for a detention hearing. Um, and past that, I just don't know yet.

CG: Michael do you have anything you want me to relay to your family, your sister or anybody else?

MC: Tell 'em I'm sorry. I've ruined their lives.

(Michael cries again. Baker thanks Michael for his cooperation. The interview is over at 10:25 A.M. He is taken out of the interrogation room.)

4

THE EMERGENCY ROOM

With Michael in custody and those of us he wounded on our way to local hospitals, there was tremendous panic outside the front of school as parents arrived, frantically looking for their children. Being the small school and community we were, word of the shooting spread rapidly by word of mouth, and my parents were probably two of the first to find out.

After Mandy left me in the lobby, she raced in a panic down the hallway and came upon Taylor. She told Taylor what happened to me, and they took off together out the doors at the end of the hall to the gymnasium. That's where most of the kids were gathered and where there was a phone Mandy could use to call our mom and dad. With cell phones not being very popular back then, that phone was pretty much Mandy's only option to get ahold of them. When Mandy and Taylor reached the phone, a pregnant student was using it, telling her mom that she and the baby's father were both OK. Taylor screamed at the top of her lungs at the girl.

"Get off the phone! Her sister's been shot! She needs to call her parents now!" The intimidated girl hung up immediately and moved out of their way. Mandy quickly dialed home. Mom answered.

"Mama! Missy was shot!" she said in such frenzy that Mom couldn't comprehend what she said. Mandy repeated herself. This time Mom understood her, so well, in fact, that she leapt from her wheelchair and moved as fast as she could down the hallway to the front door. Dad was outside with our dog.

"Ray! Ray! Mandy just called. Missy's been shot!" she shouted to him.

"She was shot?" he later said was his first thought. "How is that possible? She's at school." That's how rare school shootings were. Back then, a shooting at school was unimaginable. Today it's often a parent's worst fear.

After telling Dad, Mom spun around and ran back down the hallway to Christie's room. Christie was starting to wake up, having heard Mom yelling at Dad, but she didn't know what the furor was about. Mom flung her door open and told her what had happened.

"Go to the school and get Mandy, and we'll meet you at the hospital!" she said. Christie sprung out of bed, threw on some clothes, jumped into her car, and maneuvered the West Paducah country roads to Heath at about 90 miles per hour. With many hysterical family members of other students who lived closer to Heath having already arrived, Christie parked on the side of the road as close to the school as possible and ran the rest of the way.

It was complete chaos when she got close to the gym as parents randomly grabbed her in desperation, asking if she'd seen their daughter or son. Somehow, amid all the commotion and the sea of teenagers, Christie spotted Mandy almost immediately, grabbed her arm, and dragged her to the car. She would stop at nothing to get to the hospital.

There were two hospitals in the area: Western Baptist and Lourdes. Five of us were taken to Western Baptist and three of us to Lourdes. Christie didn't know that and had no idea where I had been taken, so she picked Lourdes because she was more familiar with that hospital. She guessed correctly. The others being taken to Lourdes were Kayce and Shelley.

On their way to the hospital, Mandy was crying and shaking. Christie said Mandy was "wide-eyed" and couldn't keep her composure. Mandy was trying to tell her what happened but was talking so quickly and was so overcome with emotion that everything out of her mouth was incoherent. Christie was finally able to calm her down enough to get a couple pieces of information out of her: Mandy didn't know if I were alive or not, and Michael was the shooter. Neither piece of information did Christie much good. She didn't know Michael, so that meant nothing to her.

The ambulance I was in was probably just a few minutes ahead of my sisters. Though I couldn't hear the siren, I'm sure it was blaring because we seemed to be traveling pretty fast, making for a jarring ride. There were two paramedics and another injured student from the shooting in the back with me. I didn't know for sure whether it was Kayce or Shelley because I couldn't see her face, but based on the attention they were giving her and knowing after the fact how critical Kayce's injury was, I have no doubt it was Kayce.

At first, one paramedic was tending to me and the other to Kayce. The one with me was standing up while the ambulance was moving and wanted to give me an IV, but because of all the bumps we hit, he struggled to keep his balance. I know this may sound strange given the grave nature of what had happened to me and others at Heath, but watching him try to hold this needle in his hand without falling over made me laugh. I remember thinking: "You think you're going to stick that needle in me when you can't even stay still your-self? I don't think so."

He eventually gave up on it and turned to help the other paramedic with Kayce. With their backs to me and blocking my view of her, I couldn't see what was going on, but by what they were saying and by their body motions, I knew they were administering CPR to her. This seemed to continue for a significant portion of the roughly 15-minute ride. I just lay there stoically and watched as they worked together to save her. If I were in any other condition, I know I would have been crying my eyes out watching them do that. But having been through what I had been through to that point, very likely I was in shock, not feeling a whole lot physically or emotionally.

Meanwhile, my parents, who left home about the same time Christie did, drove straight to Lourdes. Like Christie, they went there because they were more famil-iar with that hospital and had a hunch that's where I was taken. Though they guessed correctly, they got there so quickly that I had not yet arrived. So they guessed I must have been transported to Western Bap-tist.

They raced the two-and-a-half miles only to find, of course, that I wasn't there either. With some of the other wounded teens having arrived at Baptist and seeing that none of them were me, they returned to Lourdes, where I had just arrived. I don't know if the ambulance was slow or if my parents were fast. I would guess the latter. Their baby had been shot.

The paramedics took Kayce out of the ambulance first, then me. The emergency area looked like a scene from the TV show *ER*, except I was in it. It was complete chaos. Doctors and nurses were everywhere. Some were yelling and screaming. Others were crying because many of them had children at Heath and had no idea if their kids would be the next to be wheeled through the doors on gurneys. One team of physicians and nurses continued to give Kayce CPR. Another worked on me, giving me a chest tube and a couple of IVs.

Since my parents weren't there yet, a doctor asked me if I knew anyone who worked at the hospital, hoping someone familiar could come to comfort me in what was obviously a very tense situation. The only person I could think of was Dr. David Grimes. He was a gynecologist who worked at Lourdes and had some members of my family as his patients. Fortunately, he was there. He came and, along with Dr. Dan Howard, tended to me.

First they asked me to move my legs. I felt like I was but actually wasn't. Then they gave me a prick test, poking me in the stomach with a pin to see what I could feel.

"I can't feel anything," I told them.

They examined me further and found where the bullet had entered: through the front of me on the left side, just below my shoulder. But they didn't know if my spinal cord had been severed, nor did they know if I had been shot more than once. X-rays would help determine how severe my injuries were.

Several people somberly gathered in the waiting room: Christie, Mandy, my parents, Sissy, Dale (Sissy's husband and my uncle), my grandma, and several friends. It wasn't long before a doctor told them what he knew at that point. Then he allowed them to come in and see me.

What they found when they walked in was probably not what they expected: a girl at peace with herself and her situation. I could tell by the looks on their faces that they were worried about me and wanted to ask me questions, but they didn't. Some of them cried. I told them there was no reason to cry and that I was fine. It was almost like I was comforting them more than they were comforting me. I certainly understood why they

were so sad, but I really felt this was just the way it was
meant to be. In fact, when the doctor told me I was
paralyzed, I tried to make myself cry because I thought
it would look weird if I didn't, but I couldn't cry. I had
already accepted God's plan for the next stage of my life.
He was with me. This may sound crazy to some, but I
don't know how else to explain it.

The doctors allowed everybody to stay for a few
minutes before I was taken to X-ray. The X-rays showed
two holes: the one in the front and one in the middle of
my back and one bullet. They figured I had been shot
twice but wondered where the other bullet was. When
they moved me around a bit and lifted me up, they
found I had only been shot once. That bullet inside me
they saw on the X-ray? It wasn't inside me. It was
between my back and shirt. The front hole was where
the bullet entered. The back hole was where it exited.
And for whatever reason, it didn't go through my shirt.
The bullet had not only hit my spinal cord, but it also
punctured my left lung. One of the doctors held the
bullet up for me to see.

"Wow, that thing went through my body?" I said. It
seemed strange that it didn't have enough force to make
it through my shirt, but that's pretty much all I thought
about it. I still wasn't feeling a whole lot of emotion.
What happened had happened. Seeing the bullet didn't
move me a whole lot. After the X-rays, they took me to
the intensive care unit where I would remain for the
week.

Along with heavy doses of morphine, my diet in
ICU included ice cubes, chicken broth, beef broth, and
Jell-O. I had to be given baths in bed, if you can really
call them baths. My hair was washed with some sort of
non-rinsing shampoo. I didn't have much of an appetite
and had lost a lot of weight. About all I could do was lay
flat on my back while doctors determined the extent of
my injuries.

Their conclusion was that surgery would do no good and could possibly make my condition worse. My injury was in the upper thoracic area at the T4 level. In layman's terms, I would never again be able to feel anything below my chest. My doctor, Monte Rommelman, said my spinal cord was intact, but there were bone and metal fragments in it, making it nonfunctional. Any surgery, he said, could damage the cord more. He showed me a skeleton and explained to me what happened, though I didn't fully grasp it. All I really thought was: "Am I really going to be in a wheelchair for the rest of my life? Could it possibly be just temporary?" I didn't know and really didn't think much more about it at that time. It would be weeks before the reality of it all would hit me.

I was comforted that week in ICU with a steady stream of family and friends visiting me, including one very embarrassing visit. Christie, Pam, and her son, Winston, were there with me when a boy named John, who lived in the house behind me, walked into the room. Taylor and I used to jump on the trampoline and swim with him at Taylor's house every chance we had. Yeah, he was pretty cute. Well, as soon as John walked in, Winston felt the need to point out that the heart monitor hooked up to me was suddenly beeping at a much faster rate.

"Shut up, Winston!" I said sheepishly. Nobody, including me, even noticed it until he pointed it out. John just smiled but didn't say anything. I owed Winston one after that. Talk about an awkward moment!

That week I was allowed to have a visitor stay each night in the room with me. I don't think it was typical for the hospital to allow that in ICU, but it was clearly a unique situation. Mandy really wanted to be the one to stay with me but was in no shape emotionally to do so. She ended up sleeping in the waiting room all week, having to be dragged out at one point just to go home and take a shower.

As hurt as I was physically, Mandy suffered much more severe trauma mentally. I couldn't imagine what it must have been like for her to feel a bullet go through her hair, watch her sister collapse to the floor, see Kayce dying a few feet away from me, and witness Michael holding that gun. I wanted her to stay at my side overnight at the hospital, but there was no way she could and no way I could ask her to, so the nod went to Christie. The sister who had been like a second mother to me was filling that role again in a huge way. She pulled a chair up to my bed, held my hand the entire time she was with me and probably got no sleep whatsoever. I will always be grateful for her unconditional love and support during what was the most tumultuous week of my life.

Before my parents left Christie and me at the hospital the day of the shooting, I told my mom something that I thought might shock her – and it did. I told her that even though Michael shot me just hours earlier that day and probably paralyzed me for life, I had already forgiven him. I'm not even sure what made me tell her that. It's just the way I felt, and I thought she should know. After the initial stunned look on her face went away, her reaction was what I had expected and hoped for. She said if I could forgive him, so could she. Mom told the rest of the family.

"What? She forgave him?" Christie said to my mom with disbelief.

But Christie and the rest of the family eventually agreed with Mom: if I were able to forgive him, how could they not? I don't know that they understood my willingness to forgive him so quickly, but they accepted it.

It may sound bizarre that a 15 year old could think that way, but I did. Maybe it stemmed from my baptism less than two years earlier in the eighth grade. That momentous night in front of that congregation had strengthened my faith to the point where, as a teenager, my relationship with God was as strong as it had ever been.

Faith, hope, love, understanding, charity: I was fortunate, at such a young age, that they were all at the forefront of my life. And so was forgiveness.

5

FORGIVENESS

One reason some people have a hard time forgiving others, in my opinion, is because they fight the urge to do so. And what they're ultimately fighting, I believe, is Jesus Christ's attempt to enter their hearts.

Some think forgiveness is a sign of weakness, that forgiving someone is like saying there is nothing wrong with what that person did. But that couldn't be further from the truth. Forgiveness does not exonerate a person from responsibility or punishment for what he or she did. It's an acknowledgment that he or she did something wrong, that we realize we all make errors in judgment, and that Christ's strength and presence in our lives will shine even in the gravest moments if we open our hearts.

Michael's errors were ruthless. Nobody on earth expected me to forgive him for what he did – not even Michael. I had every right to be angry at him for the rest of my life. He robbed me of my ability to walk, murdered my friends, nearly killed my sister, and scarred so many people emotionally. What he did was solely his decision. He planned the crime and chose to commit the crime. He needed to face the consequences. Punishment was justified. But it didn't mean I couldn't forgive him. Jesus told me that day that forgiving him was what I needed to do – and I listened. I needed to do it for Michael, but more importantly, I needed to forgive him for me if I were going to get past that tragic day and make something of my life.

How did I hear Jesus' message to me that day? Actually it started many years earlier when I was a young child growing up in a loving home. No, we weren't a perfect family. It wasn't always peaceful. As close as Mandy and I have always been, we had our share of arguments. But it was through those arguments that I eventually realized being angry at people was not a pleasant experience. While our fights seemed legitimate as they were happening, once we calmed down I realized how pointless they were. I would ask myself, "Instead of being so mad at each other, why couldn't we have just talked it out?" It was far more satisfying than being angry.

People need to take the time in any heated situation to realize that they have the option of being angry or being happy. Often people say, "She makes me so mad." If someone makes us so mad, it's because we allow them to do so. A long time ago I decided that happiness was what I preferred, and it's what I've stuck with ever since. That attitude helped me forgive Michael and accept the fate God gave me.

God preaches about the importance of forgiveness throughout the Bible. In Matthew 6:14-15, he says: "For if you forgive men their trespasses, your heavenly Father will also forgive you. But if you do not forgive men their trespasses, neither will your Father forgive your trespasses."[12] In Matthew 18:21-22, he says: "Then Peter came to him and said, 'Lord, how often shall my brother sin against me, and I forgive him? Up to seven times?' Jesus said to him, 'I do not say to you, up to seven times, but up to seventy times seven.'"[13] But I think one of the most gripping Bible passages is Ephesians 4:31-32:

> "Let all bitterness, wrath, anger, clamor, and evil speaking be put away from you, with all malice. And be kind to one another, tender-hearted, forgiving one another, even as God in Christ forgave you."[14]

None of us is perfect. How many times have we done something to someone that we're not proud of? How many times have we hurt someone physically or emotionally? For example, the evening I stayed out well past curfew, I scared the heck out of my parents. I didn't think about what the consequences might be of me staying out for a couple extra hours, until I arrived home and discovered my dad was driving around town searching for me. Mom was furious and told me she'd never trust me again. Yet, in time, they forgave me.

There was a time in middle school when I decided I needed to shed some pounds. I approached it with such enthusiasm that I went from being overweight to being nearly underweight. One day after I had lost all that weight, a girl came up to me in school and asked me if I were anorexic. People used to make unflattering comments to me about being too heavy. Now this girl was saying that I was too thin? I couldn't win, and it hurt. Though she wasn't really my friend and probably didn't care how I felt about her question, I forgave her in my mind. Instead of making critical comments right back to her or saying some nasty things about her behind her back, I chose not to. Instead, I forgave her and moved on with my life.

Those examples obviously don't compare with what Michael did. Breaking curfew or teasing someone about her appearance is not murder, but the Bible does not instruct us to forgive only in certain cases. It says we need to always forgive.

As Jesus hung from the cross, he cried out, "Father, forgive them, for they do not know what they do."[15] Michael knew what he was doing as far as his plan to randomly shoot people, but he didn't give a thought to what the consequences might be. If Jesus could forgive the people who hurled stones at Him, spit on Him, and nailed Him to a cross, how could I not forgive Michael for hurting me? If we look at our own lives before judging others, we will see that forgiveness is what we all want and need. And if we let Christ in, it's something we can all do.

By letting Christ in, I was able to free my heart of any anger I had toward Michael and move forward with my life. I hoped that forgiving him had a positive effect on him. I hoped it made Michael think about what he did and made him realize that he hurt some good people who liked him. But the forgiveness was mainly for me.

After the shooting, I had so many things to worry about. I had to learn how to live all over again but without the use of my legs. Getting dressed and taking a bath were major chores. Moving from here to there took a lot of exertion. I even had to schedule my life around going to the bathroom. I simply didn't have the energy or the time to waste on him. He dictated my life on December 1, 1997, but it didn't mean he had to dictate my life every day after that. Why expend my energy on angry thoughts of him?

Over time I learned all of the good that I could make out of this situation. There were so many children who could learn from me and what I go through every day. There were causes such as finding a cure for spinal cord injuries for which I could be an outspoken advocate. People have told me that simply meeting me and seeing that I haven't let Michael's actions keep me down has been such an inspiration to them. So much good has come from such a tragic event, good that could not have happened if I hadn't forgiven him.

That same attitude, I think, helped my schoolmates at Heath go forward. Roger Palmer, a youth pastor at First Baptist Church in Paducah, used to come into the school every couple of weeks to help students work on relationship-building. He was called into Heath by several teachers and students hours after the shooting. I think he was a big reason why the kids were able to hang a sign in the school the next day that said, "We forgive you Mike!" and one outside the school that said, "We forgive you because God forgave us."

One of the signs outside the school
the day after the shooting.
(December 3, 1997, *Paducah Sun* / Kenneth Holt)

Some people who knew nothing about us condemned us for forgiving Michael so quickly. It can be difficult to comprehend how we could do that. Before the shooting, I never would have guessed we could. But it's amazing what we can do when we're put to the test. We always felt like we were opening our hearts to Christ each day in our prayer circle. Those signs the students made were proof that we were.

Does this mean everybody should forgive no matter what and as quickly as I forgave Michael? I wish I could confidently say yes to both of those questions, but I can't. I can't preach to people that they should always forgive because I haven't experienced every situation. If your child is killed by a drunk driver, should you forgive the driver? If your parents are murdered, should you forgive the murderer? If you are raped, should you forgive the rapist? I don't think anybody can answer those questions honestly without actually being in those situations.

Some people can't forgive, even if they've tried. When we look at the crimes committed against them or their loved ones, it can be difficult to argue with them. So what is my advice to someone who wants to let Christ in and forgive, but feels he or she can't or isn't sure how to do it?

First of all, we need to realize that we all heal in different ways and over different periods of time. Just because we don't feel like we can forgive someone immediately doesn't mean we can't forgive them next week, next year, or in 10 years. Perhaps not many people in my situation would have been able to forgive Michael the day of the shooting. Just because I could doesn't mean others could. It may take a while – a long while. But if we give it time and don't fight it, it can happen.

Secondly, we need to focus on ourselves and what forgiveness can do for us. Forgiving someone can lift an enormous burden off our shoulders and allow us to concentrate on our recovery. We may feel like we're being weak by absolving that person of what he or she did to us, but we're not. What we're actually doing is saying, "I'm not going to let you beat me down. I have a life to live, I'm going to live it, and you're not going to stop me."

I don't know if the families of the girls Michael killed have forgiven him. I've never lost a child or sibling, so I have no idea how I would react. Personally, I can't imagine being able to forgive in that situation. But then again, it never dawned on me that I could forgive someone for paralyzing me.

What I do know is this: if they haven't forgiven him, they could bring some peace to their lives if they could find a way to forgive. Michael so deeply hurt them. That pain will never go away. But it can be lessened.

Forgiving someone is not easy, but it's much easier than living with an angry heart. An angry heart condemns us to emotional and spiritual death.

6

GOOD-BYE JESSICA, KAYCE, AND NICOLE

There were many angry hearts after the shooting, but that anger was set aside, at least for a day, on December 5, 1997. That's when the world's attention was focused on the families of Jessica, Kayce, and Nicole, who were laid to rest. About 2,000[16] grief-stricken people, including Christie, Mandy, and Kelly Hard packed Bible Baptist Heartland Worship Center in West Paducah on a sunny, but chilly afternoon, to pay their final respects.

A photo from the *Paducah Sun*/Steve Nagy, December 6, 1997 from the funeral held for Nicole Hadley, Jessica James, and Kayce Steger.

The girls were honored at one funeral service followed by three separate burials. The service was broadcast live on CNN for those who could not attend but wanted to watch. I was one of those people as I solemnly gazed at the screen from my hospital bed in the intensive care unit with my mom at my side. I had to stare at the ceiling that first week because doctors didn't want me lifting my head yet, so they gave me special glasses with reflectors that allowed me to keep my head down and still see the television on the wall.

I was on so much morphine that I don't remember exactly when I found out the girls had died, who told me or what my immediate reaction was. I cried quietly as I watched the funeral, but it was a very surreal experience for me. The morphine played a part in that, but perhaps I was in denial of their fate because I wasn't actually at the service. I had a connection to each of the girls before they died. They were my schoolmates and were in the prayer group with me, yet I wasn't able to be at their funeral to say good-bye.

Their caskets, all white, were signed by students, teachers, and family – something I couldn't do. Their bodies were shown before the service began – something I couldn't see. And their burials were something I could only hear and read about the next day. While people grieved arm in arm that day, I couldn't be with them. My emotional state and healing process were so different from everybody else's because of what happened to me.

Because of my state of mind, I couldn't recall a lot of the funeral after I watched it, but there were some parts that stuck with me and others that I watched on tape years later that jogged my memory.

I vividly recall the Heath Choir. There were probably fifty or sixty students in it, all dressed in immaculate white gowns and singing the "Prayer of St. Francis." I have no idea how they managed to sing. The television camera panned slowly back and forth on them, and I didn't see a single one of them crying or not singing. And what a fitting song to sing with lines like "It is in pardoning that we are pardoned," and "It is in dying that we're born to eternal life."

Each family's pastor spoke. The TV station I was watching split the screen during most of each talk. On one side was the minister speaking and on the other side was a picture of the girl he was speaking about.

I recall one minister in particular. He was talking about Nicole and opened a red envelope that had been given to the Hadley family by a very courageous student at Heath Middle School. In it was a card with a message for the family. The student expressed support for them and praised them for helping save the lives of others: "It happened slow, and that's hard," the student wrote. "But you saved others with your loss, and that's what you need to keep in mind."[17]

It was pretty well publicized, as it should have been, that Nicole's family donated several of her organs.[18] That's what the student who wrote that note meant when talking about her slow death and the fact that they saved others. But Nicole's death saved others in more ways than that. There's no telling how many people in the years since, because of reading about what happened to her or hearing me or others talk about her and what happened that day, have changed their minds about committing such violent acts or had spoken up when they heard a threat, or have made changes in their lives for the better.

The caskets of the girls were spread around the front of the church, each flanked with their personal items, flowers, and lots of photos. There were a few songs played, including "How Do I Live," by LeAnn Rimes and "Amazing Grace," songs I still struggle to listen to today. Stephen Curtis Chapman, a Heath graduate and Christian music singer, also sang and played his guitar.

But what I remember the most was just thinking about the three girls as the funeral progressed, trying to picture the last time I saw them and what great people they all were.

I knew Kayce much better than Nicole and Jessica because we grew up together and were in the same grade. We weren't best friends, but we saw a lot of each other and did things together. We attended the same elementary, middle, and high schools. We were in Girl Scouts and her mom was one of our troop leaders. We were both in band: she played the clarinet. I still have a cute picture of the two of us on a field trip at the Capitol building in Frankfort and a video of her having fun during a swimming party at my house about a year-and-a-half before she was killed.

Kayce was best friends with Kelly Hard, who was one of my best friends, so we had opportunities to see and like each other. She was a member of Twelfth Street Baptist Church[19] and very devout in her faith, a very sweet person who always seemed so happy. Kayce was buried in Mount Zion Baptist Church cemetery in western McCracken County.

Jessica, two years older than me, was a very talented person with a very strong faith in God. She was in a dance group, served in church youth groups, and played French horn in the band. Though we saw each other daily in band practice, I really didn't know her that well because of our age difference. Despite that, when I give talks, I often reflect on who she was based on what those close to her have told me.

Jessica was a good, spiritual person who never took life for granted. She was prepared to meet our Lord at any time given how deep her faith was and how she dedicated her life to serving others. She led an amazing life in the short time she was here. I will never forget Jessica, and will always do everything I can to keep her legacy alive. Jessica was a member of Kevil Baptist

Church[20] and was buried at Brooks Memorial Gardens.

Nicole was a year younger than I was. She was closer friends with Taylor and Michael than she was with me, but she'd been to my house where we'd hung out together. She was also in band, and I remember her being a very intelligent and fun person. She, Taylor, and another girl used to call themselves the "Three El Caminos." She was a very good athlete and loved to play basketball. The fact that her organs were donated to save others said a lot about what good people she and her family were. Even in death, Nicole brought life to others. I only wish I had gotten to know her better before she left us. She was laid to rest in Woodlawn Memorial Garden.

Having missed the funeral, I felt fortunate to be able to pay my own tribute to the girls the following year in a couple of ways. About six months after the shooting, Mandy took me to their graves. It wasn't the same as it would have been had I been at the funeral, but I was glad to be able to at least have somewhere to go to pay my respects. I didn't cry or get emotional. With all I had been through since that day, I was past many of those emotions. But it was sad to be sitting next to their headstones in my wheelchair, thinking about what we all went through that day, sad to know that young girls my age who were so good and so innocent were never coming back. I quietly prayed at each of their graves and said good-bye.

I also paid my respects about a year after the shooting when an elaborate, outdoor memorial loaded with symbolism was constructed in the Heath courtyard and dedicated in a ceremony to those of us who died or were injured. It was a large circular shape with a brick wall all around. There were three openings in the wall for people to walk in and out of the memorial: each opening representing a girl who died. Within the circle was a pool of water with eight fountains in it, each one representing each of us who was shot. There was also a large rock in front of the fountain engraved with an angel, the names of the girls who died, and a Bible verse: "Let Not Your Heart Be Troubled: Ye Believe In God. Believe Also In Me." Around the rock was a small area of grass that had eight small rocks in it. Five of the rocks were engraved with the names of those of us who were injured. Three rocks were left blank in memory of Jessica, Kayce, and Nicole.

This memorial in the school's courtyard
was constructed to honor the
three students who died
and five who were injured.

Here is a close-up photo of the rock that is the center-piece of the memorial. Aside from that memorial, the school has a headstone with the three deceased girls' names on it that sits in the courtyard.

There is also a tabletop glass case in the lobby that has been there since right after the shooting. The table rests in front of the trophy cases, right next to the spot Michael was standing when he fired the gun. Inside it is a newspaper from the day after the funeral, a program from the memorial dedication, and some other mementos, such as a police car (Kayce hoped to be a police officer), some pictures, and some stuffed animals. On top of the table is a statue of an angel and a wire sculpture of five people holding hands in a circle, which represented our prayer group.

I've always been very pleased with the way Heath has embraced the tragedy. Administrators could have tried to sweep it under the rug by changing the look of the school and not having any memorials. I know some people probably wish they would have done that because for them, the best way to deal with the pain of that day is to not see any reminders of it. That's certainly understandable. But for me and many others, the best way to deal with the pain is to confront it, learn everything we can from it, and not forget about it. It is important for the students today to be taught or reminded about what happened that day.

If you think about it, the freshmen at Heath in the 2008-09 school year were only three or four years old when the shooting occurred. No doubt they don't remember it. Yet to those of us who lived through it, it sometimes feels like it happened just yesterday.

The students today need to know how significant that event was, not only to those who were there that day, but also to the community and the entire nation. It's part of Heath's history. It's part of our nation's history. Maybe not a pleasant part, but a part that can teach the world lessons through the deaths and injuries that day and through the strength and resiliency the school and community showed in the aftermath. As someone who survived, I feel I have a responsibility to teach some of those lessons.

Nobody understands why the lives of Jessica, Kayce, and Nicole were cut short, but the fact that three wonderful girls who did so much good here could be taken from us so soon made me realize how fortunate I was to have a second chance at life, one that I couldn't take for granted. The big question before me was: "What was I going to do with that second chance?"

7

ROAD TO RECOVERY

I left intensive care after a week. My condition had improved from critical to stable and doctors moved me to the eighth floor of Lourdes where I ate some real food and worked on regaining my strength. After a week there, I moved to physical therapy on the fifth floor where I learned to do the things in life that were once so simple: bathing, dressing, getting in and out of bed, going to the bathroom, and getting from one place to another.

Dr. Rommelman didn't mince words regarding my prognosis when he addressed the national media December 10, just after I'd been moved to the eighth floor. "It will be a matter of long-term rehabilitation for Missy with the anticipation that she will be a paraplegic. She can live a normal life, but it will be from a wheelchair," he said.[21]

While I'm sure the reaction of many people was one of sadness, I felt I was ready for that challenge, and I had plenty of support not only from those who knew me, but from complete strangers around the world. I received thousands upon thousands of cards and letters, many accompanied with generous gifts of cash or toys. Mom sat next to my bed and opened and read every one of them. She had opened so many that one night while we were eating dinner, she accidentally used the letter opener to butter her roll!

The most letters I got in one day was 600. Another day there were 500. They kept coming and coming to the hospital, my house and my church and not just from this country, but from as far away as Australia and Zimbabwe. I was overwhelmed with emotion. It meant so much to me that people I knew were helping in any way possible, but to think that thousands of people who never met me and likely never would meet me took time out of their days to send me good wishes was unreal. Yes, Michael's actions that day had affected people across the nation, but I had no idea how much they had affected the world and to what extent. To me, it was all an affirmation of how much love there really is on this planet. One person did a terrible thing to me, but thousands came to my aid.

One card that struck me as so sweet was from a family in a foreign country I'd never even heard of before. Nearly the entire letter was written in their native language, but they also wrote a few statements they knew in English such as "We pray." I'm sure they knew that I wouldn't be able to read their language, but they sent it anyway because they cared, and it truly brightened my day. I got tons of cards from children, many of them with adorable drawings of a person in a wheelchair. There were also many gifts.

One group of children from out of state actually drove all the way to the hospital to give me a laptop computer they'd bought with money they raised. Through the mail I received a Game Boy, Dutch dolls from Holland, necklaces from Hawaii, a card signed by the 1998 Kentucky Wildcats championship basketball team, personal cards from President Clinton, stuffed animals, hand-made quilts and money.

I had no idea how much cash was coming in. Mom would say, "Oh you received $20" or "They enclosed $50." When a tragedy strikes someone, even strangers wonder what they can do to help. Sometimes they feel that giving a few dollars won't do much good, but I can say from experience that it does. Every penny that came in was put into a fund for me to use solely for medical purposes such as physical therapy, medication and equipment needs. I use the money from that fund regularly today for those needs, and the hope is that it will last the rest of my life. With all of the challenges I've faced – and will continue to face – since the shooting, it's been a blessing knowing that the financial aspect is something I hopefully will not have to worry about. I was and will be forever grateful to the thousands of people around the world who made that possible.

I was still initially on morphine when I arrived on the eighth floor, so I didn't feel a whole lot of emotion when I got there, though a change of scenery was nice. The door to my new room was basically a revolving one with visitors constantly coming and going. Many hospital patients prefer not to be bothered by people, but I was the complete opposite. There were times when the hospital staff would end the visiting hours for a while just to give me a chance to rest, but I didn't want them to. The more people who came, the better I felt. Of course my family visited daily, and Christie or someone else continued to spend the night in my room.

Three very significant visits from people outside of my family that I remember were from our principal, Mr. Bond; a girl I hadn't talked to since middle school whom I wasn't friends with anymore; and Michael's parents, John and Ann Carneal.

When Mr. Bond came in, he was immediately over-whelmed with emotion and cried when he saw me. I wasn't surprised at his reaction, though I felt he certainly had no reason to feel that way. Perhaps he thought that because he was the principal of our school, it was his role to be our protector at all times. Perhaps he felt like he had failed me and the other kids for what Michael had done. But he didn't fail us.

What could he have done? He didn't know what Michael was plotting. There was nothing Michael had done in the past to indicate to Mr. Bond that he might do this. If Mr. Bond had known, he would have stopped it before it started. That is why when I talk to school children today, I plead with them to tell somebody in authority when they hear another student talking about doing something violent. In my opinion, it's better to be called a tattletale than to end up dead or in a wheelchair.

I don't really remember what Mr. Bond and I talked about, just small talk, I guess. But I do recall that the longer he stayed, the happier he became. He may have realized that I was doing fine and that I was going to be able to handle this. He may always feel some guilt for what happened to me and the other students, but he shouldn't. No school principal would have been able to stop Michael that day.

Another visitor was a girl I went to high school with but hadn't talked to since middle school. We were good friends in middle school but, after she became close friends with another girl, we drifted apart. We probably hadn't spoken in at least two years when, out of the blue, she walked into my hospital room. We didn't really have much to talk about, as one might imagine. It was pretty awkward. I can't even say I was very thrilled at first that she came, but my attitude softened after I realized she didn't have to come at all. The fact that she did said a lot. We may not have been friends anymore, but her visit showed that she still cared about me. It's a shame that we don't always treat people well and that it sometimes takes a tragic event to make us realize the importance of always loving others and being kind to people. She and I haven't talked to each other since, but that's OK. We went our separate ways and life went on for both of us. But the fact that I had hundreds of visits from people and can remember hers shows what an impact her presence that day had on me.

The most memorable visit that week was from Mr. and Mrs. Carneal. They had called my parents ahead of time and asked them if they could visit me. My parents asked me how I felt about that. I told them I didn't mind at all.

When they came in, I was my usual happy self with a smile on my face, hoping to diffuse any tension there might be, but the Carneals were crying and looked absolutely devastated. Mrs. Carneal had made me some little scrunchies to tie my hair back. That relieved the anxiety, at least for a moment, but it didn't really change their moods. It was a bit uncomfortable because there wasn't a whole lot we could say to each other. They said they were sorry for what happened, but that was the only reference either of us made to the shooting. Michael was never a topic of conversation. I continued to smile and tried to make them feel at ease, but I don't think it really worked. The visit lasted just a few minutes.

I felt sorry for the Carneals. I know they thought it was their fault. They felt so helpless and would have done anything to turn back time if they could. Their son had committed such a horrible crime, yet several people blamed them for it as much as they blamed Michael. I thought that was unfair. What Michael did was not a true reflection on them as parents, in my opinion. Mrs. Carneal was always involved at school. Mr. Carneal was a well-respected attorney who also volunteered at school and provided the financial support for his family. Their daughter was well liked and very bright, the valedictorian of her class. God was a part of their family life. What happened with Michael was a mystery to everyone, even to them. I wonder if, for whatever reason, they just didn't connect with Michael like they did with their daughter. That happens between a lot of parents and their teenage children.

Young children love to talk, but once they hit their teen years, the communication often stops. They have a lot on their minds: the opposite sex, changes in their body, peer pressure. Sadly, their parents are often the last ones they go to for help. I felt close to my parents and didn't have a problem talking to them about anything, but I was probably an exception. That disconnect happens in a lot of families during those formative years. It's imperative that parents reach out and try to communicate more than they ever had to before to know what is happening in their children's lives, what they're thinking, who their friends are, and what their interests are. But even then, if there is no cooperation from the teen, it can be difficult to make a connection.

While the Carneals were wishing they could help me, I was wishing I could help them. But we all knew the reality was that we'd have to go our own ways and take care of ourselves. I was grateful, though, that they had the courage to come and visit me. It made me feel good that they cared.

When they left, they apologized to my parents. My parents appreciated that and showed no animosity toward the Carneals, but they didn't have much more to say. Mom just told Mrs. Carneal, "You get that boy some help."

As much as I enjoyed all the love and attention I got on the eighth floor from all the people who came to see me, the reality was that in between those visits I was in a lot of agony. For the first few days there I still had the chest tube that was inserted the day of the shooting to drain fluid from my left lung. It went in the side of my body, through my ribs and to my lung. There was a box at the end of my bed into which the fluid drained. It was all very gross, and Mandy made it even more gross when she kept accidentally kicking that box when she walked by it.

"Mandy, stop it! That's attached to my lung!" I'd yell at her. Of course she was sorry, but that tube was just another example of the frustrations with which I had to deal.

After the tube was removed the middle of that week, the nurses had me spend time each day sitting up in a reclining chair for 30 minutes at a time to prepare me for my move to physical therapy on the fifth floor. That was the first time I had sat up since the shooting. After doing nothing but lying down for more than a week, my head and stomach weren't liking it one bit. Sitting up was painful and made me very tired and sick. I got fevers and was dizzy. My stomach turned. My blood pressure dropped.

When that happened, nurses took my temperature, stuck me with a needle to take my blood, then I'd throw up. It was a vicious cycle that went on for a couple days. As much of an accomplishment as it was to be able to sit up, and while it got easier each time I did it, I didn't want to do it anymore. It was the worst feeling in the world, and I wanted to stay in bed forever, but I knew that was not an option.

The evenings were no better. That's when I had a few anxiety attacks. The attacks could have been due in part to the fact that I was slowly being taken off the morphine, but perhaps simply having been confined to a bed for more than a week had a lot to do with them, too. During the attacks I had the feeling that I wanted to get up but couldn't. They felt like those frustrating dreams where I wanted to run but was stuck in one spot. Nurses still gradually took me off the morphine but gave me some other medication to calm my nerves. It helped, but those loved ones who stayed with me those evenings didn't get a wink of sleep.

I also had the unpleasant experience of being hooked up with a catheter (a tube that's connected to a bag that catches the urine) to drain my bladder. As I would discover once I got to physical therapy the following week, going to the bathroom would be a difficult and unpleasant experience for the rest of my life, and it would involve a catheter each day. But the catheter did lend to one funny story on the eighth floor. I was sound asleep when I was awakened in the middle of the night by some commotion at the bottom of my bed. I saw two nurses under my covers with a flashlight. I thought, *What the heck is going on?*

It turned out they were trying to get a catheter in me without waking me up. The only danger, as one of them soon realized, was that a paraplegic has no control over the muscle spasms in her legs. As one of the nurses was trying to get the catheter in, my legs slammed shut on her head. The spasms had kicked in and clamped on her like the Jaws of Life. She and the other nurse were fighting my legs, trying to pry them off her. I couldn't do anything about it other than lie there and watch. I was so embarrassed, but it was funny. Fortunately, the nurse escaped unharmed.

Toward the end of that week I was feeling a lot better. I was getting used to the reclining chair and wasn't feeling as sick when I used it. The anxiety attacks were under control. In fact, I felt good enough to finally speak to the media.

The media frenzy when the shooting occurred was like something out of a movie. Satellite trucks, reporters, videographers, and photographers from across the country descended upon Paducah. There seemed to be a story on the national news every evening. Mandy had to have police officers escort her to the girls' funerals. Christie had a TV camera rudely shoved in her face one day when she left the hospital. Another day, when doctors wheeled me from one building to another, they had two security officers flanking me. I thought it was hilarious that they felt I needed body guards, until we got outside and were literally being chased by reporters.

I had turned down reporters' requests for interviews the previous week but finally decided it was a good time to talk. Based on the cards, letters, TV coverage, and visitors to my room, I knew people wanted to know how I was doing. It would be a good opportunity to thank the public for all of their support. I spoke to a reporter from the *Paducah Sun* newspaper and allowed a photographer to take some pictures. It was a very upbeat interview, and it felt good to talk about everything. It would be the first of many interviews I would do in upcoming months – from *Dateline NBC* to *Oprah*. But despite all of that attention, I knew I had to keep my focus on getting healthy. My next grueling challenge awaited me: physical therapy.

The eighth floor was difficult, and I was glad to leave it. It served its purpose – allowing me to get a little bit of my strength back, but I had no idea when I first got there just how difficult it would be. The chest tube, fevers, vomiting, and anxiety attacks were more than I expected to have to deal with.

The next six weeks were spent on the fifth floor in physical therapy learning how to become independent again, but with several limitations. No more throwing on clothes in two minutes. No more going to the bathroom the way everyone else did. Getting in and out of bed would be a difficult chore. And a wheelchair would be my mode of transportation. On top of the physical challenges, I had some emotional ones looming: my mom's birthday, my 16th birthday, Mandy's 16th birthday, and Christmas. I'd celebrate all of them in the next week, but from my hospital bed.

There was no doubt that the support was there for me to continue. I wasn't alone. I had God, family, friends, strangers, and an outstanding hospital staff all on my side, but it was still going to be a fight. And my first battle – a severely emotional one – arose on one of my first days in physical therapy when Mandy came into my room with some completely unexpected news.

8

LEARNING TO LIVE AGAIN

We've all likely had a moment where we've become frustrated about something and abruptly had an emotional breakdown. After two long weeks of maintaining my composure fairly well and generally being buoyant about my situation, my emotions got the better of me on December 16th.

Two issues triggered them. One was that it was my mom's birthday. I know Mom didn't care where she spent her birthday or under what circumstances, as long as she was with her family. But I still felt awful that she had to spend it sitting in a hospital worrying about her daughter's well-being. The bigger matter for me, though, occurred when Mandy came into my room that morning with some unexpected news:

"Shelley's going home today," she said.

Shelley Schaberg was a couple years older than me. I didn't really know her while at Heath, but I knew of her. Everybody at Heath did because she was such an incredible athlete and nice person. Of the five of us who were injured, I got the worst of it physically but Shelley was a close second. She suffered nerve damage so severe that it ended her dream of playing college basketball.

But Shelley also refused to let the shooting keep her down. She worked hard at rehabilitation, switched her focus to soccer and went on to have a successful college career in the sport at Morehead State University.

So what was my issue with her going home? Well, it wasn't so much that she was leaving, it was that I wasn't going with her. I was truly happy for her and glad that she had recovered well enough to leave the hospital, but I knew I wouldn't be going anywhere anytime soon. Though we didn't previously know each other, Shelley had come from her room at Lourdes a couple times to visit me, and that felt so good.

As much as I loved and needed all the support I received from everyone around the world and from all the family and friends who visited me, there was something comforting about knowing that there was someone else in the hospital – someone from Heath – who suffered a similar fate and was putting up the same fight I was. It was like we were unofficially in it together, but not anymore.

"Why can't I go home?" I sobbed after Mandy told me the news. "I want to crawl into my own bed at home and just stay there! I'm tired of this! I'm done!"

For those who wondered if I were even human because of the lack of emotion I had displayed up to that point, let me tell you, the tear ducts were working hard at that moment. The flare-up lasted several minutes. I cried, and I cried hard. So many thoughts ran through my mind: the horrific sounds of the shots fired, the immense chaos that ensued in the lobby, the drive to the hospital, all the doctors and nurses working on and around me when I got there, the girls' deaths, the funerals. I showed some emotion at the time of each of those actions, but probably less than the average person would have.

I never really felt at any point during the first two weeks that I was suppressing my feelings, but maybe I was and didn't know it. It just took something unexpected, such as Shelley leaving, to trigger them.

Besides Mandy, my parents and Christie were there that day. They let me get it all out, told me that I was going to be fine, and that I would triumph in the end. I knew I would because I really had no other choice. If I was going to be independent again, I had to keep up the fight. But the outburst felt good – really good. Fifteen days of pent-up frustrations had been released. It was probably some of the best therapy I ever had. By the end of the day I felt like I was back on track mentally and ready to move forward. And looking back on it, the timing of letting those emotions flow couldn't have been better.

That's because the following week, on December 24, Mandy and I turned 16. We celebrated our birthdays and Christmas on Christmas Eve with family and friends in a conference room at the hospital. While that wasn't the ideal place to be celebrating our births and the birth of our Lord, we made it into a festive occasion by eating dinner together, exchanging gifts, and having cake. Had I not let those feelings out the week before, I'm afraid I would have on Christmas Eve, a more significant time in my life with even more people there with me.

Yes, I missed the wonderful Christmas traditions we'd had the first 15 years of my life: a birthday party and gift exchange on Christmas Eve at our house, dinner at Sissy's house on Christmas day, and Mandy and I staying in our rooms until Mom and Dad placed all the presents under the tree. It was always a fun and memorable time. We wouldn't get to do any of that this year, but we did what we could to make it as customary as possible, and we did a pretty good job of it. Nobody cried. Nobody complained about the awkwardness of the situation. Yeah, it was different, but what mattered to everyone was that we were all together.

God had once again, as He had done every year of my life previously, bestowed his blessings upon us over the Christmas season. Some outside our family may not have felt like we were very blessed because of the shooting, but we indeed felt blessed. As tragic as my situation was, there were three families that didn't have their daughters or sisters anymore. I knew I was fortunate to be alive, as did everyone else. I was given another chance at life, and it was time for me to take advantage of it.

I had my own room in physical therapy. On a typical day I woke up at about 9 A.M. and ate breakfast. One of the therapists then came to take me to one of my therapy sessions, which lasted 30 minutes or so, depending what it was we were working on. Then I returned to my room and watched television or played with my new laptop, ate lunch, attended another therapy session, returned to my room and watched more television, and then ate dinner. My family arrived late in the afternoon each day and stayed until the evening, with one of them usually spending the night with me.

Being on that floor was a bit strange for me because I was the only spinal cord injury patient there, and the closest person to my age was someone in his late 30s who had suffered head injuries. Virtually everybody else was a senior citizen who had suffered a stroke. That made me feel a bit uneasy trying to socialize because many of them had difficulty communicating. They either couldn't speak or had mental injuries. I did leave my room sometimes, usually at breakfast or lunch, and made a few friends. But for the most part, if I wasn't in therapy, I stayed in my bed.

Right away the therapists got me started with lifting weights and learning how to sit up. Because I was paralyzed from the chest down, I couldn't just raise myself up like everybody else when I was lying down. I needed to use my arms, which is why they had me lift weights. Though my arms weren't paralyzed, they were extremely weak because I hadn't used them much in more than two weeks. I could have just grabbed the bed rails to sit up, and I did initially. But with no rails on my bed at home, I needed to learn how to get up without them. To do that, I had to use my elbows by digging them into the bed and pushing up with my hands. It was very difficult at first. I struggled because I didn't have much strength, but I worked on it and lifted the weights every day. And every day it became easier to do.

A couple other early activities they had me work on were keeping my balance while in a sitting position, and transferring myself from one place to another using a board. Most people don't think about this, but an able-bodied person uses her trunk – the stomach area – to balance when she is sitting down. But what does someone like me do when she can't feel her stomach? I had to find another part of my body with which to balance, and with everything from my chest down paralyzed, I learned to balance using my head.

The best way to explain it would be to picture standing on both of your feet. When standing up, your feet give you your balance. But what happens when you lift one foot in the air? With that foot no longer on the floor and serving no purpose in balancing yourself, you need to find another way to balance, such as extending your arms out to your sides. Ever done that before? It's the same concept for me when sitting down. Without any feeling in the trunk area, something else has to provide that balance. It was difficult to learn. The therapists held objects out for me to try to grab without falling over. It took a while to master it, but I eventually did with a lot of practice.

After that, they had me practice sliding from one place to another, namely, from my bed to a wheelchair, and vice versa using a plastic, rectangular board. I did that by getting myself into a sitting position, sliding a board under by butt, balancing myself, then sliding on that board. Once I got to where I needed to go, I'd remove the board from under me. That exercise wasn't very difficult to do because so much of it was about balance, which I had already learned.

By this point I was feeling really good about what I had accomplished. It was exasperating at times, but it wasn't too bad because I could feel myself progressing each day. I had three more challenges, though, waiting for me before my six weeks in physical therapy were up: using a wheelchair, dressing myself, and going to the bathroom.

My initial reaction when I got into a wheelchair? I'm free! The first thing I did was wheel myself down to the cafeteria. I don't even know if I ate anything. I just loved the fact that I could sit up in bed, balance myself, slide myself into the chair with a board, and go wherever I wanted on my own. I was learning to become independent again. The therapy was quickly paying off.

The chair I used was manual, the same type I still use today and plan to always use. The therapists insisted I use a manual one, and I had no qualms with that. A motorized chair might have been easier and less strenuous, but I didn't need it. I was just 16 years old. Even though I didn't have the use of my legs, I was still growing and getting stronger. Learning to use it was taxing, as was evidenced by the abundance of scratches and dings I left on the hospital walls. But as with everything else they taught me to that point, I quickly got the hang of it in no time with practice.

Getting dressed was my next challenge. They started teaching me using lightweight sweat pants because they were much thinner and more flexible than jeans. How difficult could it be to put on a pair of those? How about 45 minutes of pure frustration! That's how long it took the first time I tried. The way I learned was they wrapped Velcro around each ankle that attached to handles near my knees. I had to pull the handles to try to get my legs as close to me as possible, then push my legs back down into the pants. It was the same process with putting on socks and shoes. Being five feet, eight inches tall with a lot of that height in my legs, none of this was easy. And when you throw in the fact that my legs were dead weight that worked against me by going into spasms whenever they felt like it, you can imagine how rough it was.

I also had to figure out how to put on my shirt. Though I wasn't paralyzed above my chest, the issue once again was that balancing act. Trying to put a shirt over my head, which is the body part I use to balance myself, was tricky. I figured out the easiest way to do that was by lying down. Putting a shirt over my head while on my back was a challenge, but eliminating the balancing aspect of it made it much simpler.

And then there was the matter of going to the bathroom. Until this time, the nurses were the ones taking care of my bladder and bowel issues. But no more. When I found out that I was going to have to do for myself what they had been doing for me, I was in denial.

"Are you serious?" I said. "I have to do this for the rest of my life?"

I guess I'd never thought of how a paralyzed person went to the bathroom. But with no feeling in that part of the body, it was obvious that it wasn't going to be as simple as sitting on the toilet and going. Not even close.

For my bladder, I had to learn how to use a catheter. Though I don't use a mirror now, I did when I first learned so that I could see what I was doing. Once the tube reaches the right spot in the bladder, the urine starts flowing. It took me a while to figure out how much my bladder could hold and how often I had to "cath," as I call it. Generally, I have to do it every five hours. If I wait much longer, I'll sometimes get chills or a headache. Those are a couple warning signs that I'd better cath pretty soon or I'll wet myself. While I've gotten used to doing it and can do it rather rapidly now, it can still cause a lot of problems. The bladder is very susceptible to foreign objects. Even by washing my hands and using sterilized gloves, I'm prone to a lot of bladder infections, of which I've had several.

Cleaning my bowels is even more difficult. The problem there is that by being paralyzed, I can't push it out like someone who is not paralyzed. The brain just can't get through to that area of the body. I'll sometimes get chills in my back when I have to go, but I can't just go sit on the toilet to take care of it. So what do I have to do? Clean it out myself by putting on gloves, reaching in and pulling it out manually.

When I first heard that, I couldn't believe it and refused to do it. In fact, since the nurses had also shown Mandy and Christie how to do it, I made them do it for me the first few months. Eventually, Mandy and Christie told me that it was something I had to do on my own – and I knew that. But it was, and still is, a very difficult procedure. I have to do it every other day, and it takes me about an hour each time.

Going to the bathroom is the worst part of my disability. I have to schedule my life around long bathroom breaks, and that drives me crazy. And if I know I'll be busy or out for a long time, I wear Depend underwear just in case I have an accident. It's hard for some people to understand that part of my life, but it's who I am now. It's part of being a paraplegic, and something that I have no choice but to accept and deal with.

Before I left physical therapy and Lourdes Hospital for good, there were two pretty fun things I got to do. One was appear on *Dateline NBC*. That was the first of several talk shows or news magazine shows that I would be on. They basically spent an evening following me around as I did my therapy. It was kind of strange to me that they were so interested in my story because it had been nearly two months since the shooting but, evidently, there was still a lot of curiosity from the general public about how I was doing. Though I had been a very shy person before the shooting, I decided to come out of my shell during that interview. I'm not exactly sure why. Maybe it was because I had already told the story to the local newspaper and had also gone over it all in my head several times that it just got easier to talk about. Whatever the reason, I was learning that as much as the physical therapy was helping me, the interviews were the healthiest way for me to deal with my situation mentally.

The other fun thing I got to do was go see a movie. They allowed me to go out for a day toward the end of my stay so I could see *Titanic* with Christie and Mandy. The theater we went to was not handicap accessible, so I had to sit in my wheelchair in the aisle of the theater. People bumped into me at least ten times throughout the movie because of where I was sitting and because it was so dark. It was kind of embarrassing and I wasn't real comfortable with it, but it wasn't like I was going to leave. Though we had to go back to the hospital right after the movie, it felt good to get out for those few hours. It also gave me a taste of what life was going to be like out in public. Even something once so simple, such as going to a movie, wasn't going to be simple anymore. My eyes were opening up to those things that I used to take for granted. Once I checked out of the hospital, it was going to be a different world for me.

I checked out of Lourdes the first week of February. I wish I could have thanked every person who crossed my path while I was there, from the courageous paramedics who rushed me to the hospital to all the wonderful doctors and therapists who treated me. I don't know where I would be today without everything they did for me. But my work was far from over.

I had to head to Cardinal Hill Rehabilitation Hospital
in Lexington, Kentucky, about 250 miles northeast of
Paducah, for a little more than two months of advanced
rehabilitation. There I would do more strenuous exercises
and learn to take my own showers. I would even learn
how to jump curbs and do wheelies in my wheelchair. I
would meet people like me who were in wheelchairs
because of various accidents. It would be a chance for
me to talk to them, teach them, learn from them, and see
where I was at in relation to them as far as my abilities.

But it was not going to be easy. No more sleeping in.
No more lounging around in my room. No more people
spending the night. Cardinal Hill would be the toughest
test for me yet. It was very difficult at times but, by that
point, I didn't expect anything for the rest of my life to
be easy.

9

From Boot Camp to Heath

For the first time since I ran out the front door two months earlier to catch a ride to school with Carrie and Taylor, I was back home – for an hour. I checked out of Lourdes one morning the first week of February 1998 and, by doctors' orders, had to be at Cardinal Hill that evening. They didn't want any gaps in my rehabilitation. We stopped at home just long enough for Christie, Mandy, and my parents to pack some clothes. They were going to rent an apartment near the hospital to be close to me.

Mom was always a stay-at-home mom and Dad was retired, so missing work was not an issue for them. Christie, who had come home in the fall from the University of Kentucky to attend Paducah Community College, had already made up her mind that she was going wherever I was going. Her education, she decided, could wait. And Mandy? Well, she did go back to school for a couple days in December to take finals and had every intention of continuing, but on her way to school with Carrie and Taylor the first day back after Christmas break, they were hit by another car. Can you believe her

luck? None of them were injured, but Mandy had
enough.

"That's it!" she cried after the accident. "I want to go
home!" And she did. She felt jinxed. That was probably
her fourth day of school in a month, and two of those
days consisted of a bullet flying through her hair and a
car accident. Being with me was where she felt safest,
and my parents granted her that wish. She was with me
every day at Lourdes and would be with me every day
in Lexington. The next time she would go back to school
would be with me in May.

For the hour we were at home I sat in the living
room, watched TV, and played with my cat, Tippi, and
dog, Nick. I looked around the room and realized something I had never noticed before: our house was rather
small. It was a ranch with three bedrooms and one
bathroom. It never used to seem that small to me, but
now that Mom and I were both in wheelchairs, it felt
cramped. I figured when we got home from Lexington
we'd have to get rid of some furniture or move some
stuff around so we could maneuver our way through
the house.

Though the visit was short, it was nice to be home.
Tippi and Nick were coming with us to Lexington, and
I was actually looking forward to the trip. It was not
only a chance for me to continue my rehabilitation but,
having lived in Paducah my entire life, the thought of
living in another city for a couple months was pretty
exciting.

We got to Lexington in the evening. It was dark and
there was snow on the ground, something we hadn't
seen much of in Paducah that winter. I'd been to
Lexington once before. It was the previous summer to
see some fireworks on the Fourth of July. Of course, I'd
never been to Cardinal Hill. As far as hospitals go,
Lourdes was very nice and comfortable, but Cardinal
Hill was even better. My room was huge and had a big,

beautiful, half-circle window. The only thing I didn't like was that the television could only get three channels. But as long as I had company, that would be fine. There was plenty of room for Christie or Mandy to sleep there with me, or so I thought.

Once I got settled, the nurses said it was time for everyone to leave for the evening. I asked who was going to stay with me. I didn't like the answer I got.

"Nobody," one of the nurses told me. "No visitors are allowed to stay."

She had to be kidding, I thought. But I quickly realized by the serious look on her face that it was no joke. I was stunned at first. Then I burst into tears. They were actually going to make me sleep in this big room in this strange hospital by myself? Keep in mind that I had never been alone. Mandy and I were inseparable growing up. It may sound crazy that a 16-year-old girl couldn't stand the thought of being by herself in a room, but Mandy and I shared a room at home every day of our lives. Someone always stayed with me at Lourdes. And now I suddenly wasn't allowed to have anybody in this strange place?

Since the day of the shooting, someone close to me had always been right there at my side 24 hours a day: a teacher, a family member, a friend, but not anymore. It was killing me that they were doing this to me, and I know it really hurt Mom to see me cry, but there was nothing anybody could do. It was a hospital rule and, as I would figure out later, it was part of the rehabilitation process of making me learn how to become independent. About the best I could get out of the whole deal was for the nurses to leave my door open so I could have some light from the hallway. I took what I could get. It wasn't much, but it helped me not feel so alone and scared. Eventually I calmed down and was able to fall asleep.

If that welcome to Cardinal Hill weren't enough of a shock, things didn't get any better the next morning. At Lourdes I could sleep as late as I wanted. At Cardinal Hill the nurses came in that first morning at seven o'clock. I couldn't believe it.

"What? I have to get up?" I asked incredulously. "It's too early!"

They would have none of that attitude. They insisted I get up. But I wasn't done battling.

"I'd rather just have breakfast in my room," I said, ready to roll back over and catch a few more winks before my breakfast got there. I don't know who I thought I was, but I quickly found out I wasn't important enough to do whatever I wanted to do. They got my clothes for me, but made me get myself dressed. Breakfast was in the cafeteria, and it was *now*, they told me emphatically.

Compared to Lourdes, Cardinal Hill seemed like boot camp, and I didn't like it one bit.

They wheeled me down to the cafeteria, and the way the patients there were conversing, it seemed like they all knew each other well. The therapist introduced me to everybody, then found me a place at a table to wheel my chair up to. There were probably about 15 patients, and I was the youngest. Almost all of them were in wheelchairs, and several were able to function less than I could.

There was an older man who was paralyzed from the waist up, something I had never heard of before. He had a rare disease that took away his ability to use everything except his legs, something that made me realize how lucky I was. In my mind, being able to move my arms was more important than having use of my legs because I could take care of myself easier.

There was another man there, about sixty years old, who had an accident that confined him to a wheelchair. His story turned out to be so tragic because his wife left him while he was in the hospital and, from what I had heard from others after I left Cardinal Hill, he eventually killed himself. The position I was put in by the shooting was difficult, but I couldn't imagine having to learn life all over again at his age. I only wish there had been something I could have done for him.

One man I was able to help was in his forties. A tree had fallen on him, making him a paraplegic like me. But there was a big difference between us: our attitudes. He had the most negative outlook on life of anyone I'd ever met. It made me sad that he was like that because I was just happy to be alive, so I tried my best to help him. I talked to him every chance I could. I learned that he had a wife and child who loved him very much. I told him to be happy that he had them and to be positive about life. I bought him a stress ball he could grip when he became angry to let him know someone cared about him.

Being a paraplegic didn't mean his life was over, just that his life was different. I wanted him to understand what he had, not what he didn't have. It was a lot of work on my part, but it was worth it. He told my mom one day that I had helped him so much simply by showing an interest in him and his well-being. It made me feel so good that I had helped changed his perspective.

My best friend at Cardinal Hill, though, was an 18-year-old boy named Rob Pedigo. Rob was in a car accident around January 5, just a little more than a month after the shooting. The accident left him blind, and he had one of those halos over his head to keep him stabilized. His mom had to come in each day to help him eat. The accident left him in pretty bad shape, but he was able to maintain a pretty good attitude and sense of humor.

We had one funny experience when we were hanging out in Rob's room one day, something we did pretty regularly. He loved to drink tea and he asked his mom to get him some. As soon as she left, the phone on the table next to his bed rang. We were both in our wheelchairs and he asked me to answer it, but I needed to get around him to do that. He tried to get out of my way but was having a hard time of it, and I had my chair turned in a way that I couldn't get over there. So then I tried to direct him where to go, but I was still too much in his way. We were like out-of-control bumper cars as we tried to maneuver around each other. By the time we got to the phone, it stopped ringing. Fortunately we were both able to see the humor in it and laughed about it. We knew that was another little thing that we would each have to deal with throughout our lives. But it also made me realize how much more fortunate I was than him. I couldn't imagine not having my sight. The obstacles he had to cross were so much more difficult than mine.

It didn't take long for my attitude about Cardinal Hill to change. All it took was for me to meet those people and see the disabilities with which they had to deal. Unlike at Lourdes, where those in physical therapy were so much older and most often stroke victims, the patients at Cardinal Hill were much younger and many were in wheelchairs like me. I had a new perspective. So what if I had to get up early? So what if the television in my room only had three channels? So what if I couldn't have someone stay with me? I was learning to live again. That's why I was there, and I was going to make the most of it.

A typical day for me after waking up and eating breakfast in the cafeteria was to go for some rigorous therapy until lunchtime. Mandy usually came to see me about that time and, after lunch, watched me do more work until about three o'clock. After a month, I started swimming in the late afternoon, which lasted until almost dinner time each day. The evenings were my own time. That's when the rest of my family came to visit me. We talked or watched television until visiting hours were over.

My therapy consisted of a lot of aerobics, lifting weights, transferring from my bed to my wheelchair to another chair using a plastic board so I could shower each day, standing in a frame that pulled me up and helped me to stand for a while to keep the muscles and bones in my lower body strong, and wheelies – balancing myself on the two back wheels of my chair.

The purpose of the wheelies was to learn to balance for those times when I would have to enter places that didn't have ramps, forcing me to go up curbs. It was an extremely difficult task to learn. They strapped a belt to my chair and walked behind me to catch me if I fell. I had to start at my room and wheel myself all the way to the cafeteria on my back two wheels. If my front wheels dropped to the floor, I had to go back to my room and start over. I did it every single day. It was by far the most difficult therapy I had to do at Cardinal Hill, but well worth it. The physical limitations were diminishing. The more I learned, the more independent I became.

While I gradually mastered the physical skills, I still had some mental obstacles I had to face, including one in particular that I'll never forget.

It was on March 24, 1998. That was the day of the first school shooting since Paducah. It was at Westside Middle School in Jonesboro, Arkansas. Two boys named Mitchell Johnson, 13, and Andrew Golden, 11, shot and killed four students and a teacher. They also wounded nine other students and a teacher. Golden had pulled the school's fire alarm, then ran into the nearby woods where Johnson was waiting with guns and ammunition. The boys then opened fire on the unsuspecting teachers and students, who thought that running out of the building would be their sanctuary.[22]

I couldn't believe it when I heard it. That was the third school shooting in our country in six months. Even though I was a victim in one, it still didn't seem real. Why were kids doing this? Why did they think killing was the answer? That's what many students at Westside wondered. Soon after the shooting, I appeared from Cardinal Hill via satellite on the *Montel Williams Show* to talk to some of the Westside kids who were in New York on Montel's show. They were looking to me for advice. All I could tell them was that it would take time to get past it, but that at some point they would be able to. I told them to not hold it in and that it was better to talk about it as much as they could, at least that's what I found worked for me.

Even talking to them that day was therapeutic for me. The memories of Jonesboro would never go away for them, but I felt the best thing they could do for themselves was to be open about how that tragedy made them feel and face it together.

Aside from that, my progress gradually continued. In fact, I was doing so well that I allowed some Lexington television stations to interview me and follow me around the hospital. Then came *Dateline NBC* again. Then the *Today Show*. Then *Good Morning America*. At first the other patients really didn't pay attention to what was going on, but then they realized that I was becoming somewhat of a mini-celebrity and thought it was kind of cool. It honestly didn't mean much to me to be on television. I was just enjoying the mentally therapeutic effects that talking about my condition and progress to the media was having on me and hoping my message was helpful to others.

After one of those shows aired, I got a visit in April from a minister I'd never met before named Tim Richardson. He was with the Church of Christ in Lexington; he showed up unexpectedly one day. He came to talk to me about my condition and offer me support, but he also had another reason for coming. He had noticed, when one of those news shows aired a segment about me, that I had a poster on my wall of the Backstreet Boys. They were my favorite boy band at the time, but I really didn't know why that meant anything to him until he revealed the connection.

"You know Kevin Richardson in the band?" he asked me.

Of course I did.

"Well, he's my brother," he said with a big smile.

I couldn't believe it! He was there to not only talk to me as a minister and offer his spiritual support, but he had free tickets and backstage passes for Mandy, Christie, and me to one of their upcoming summer concerts! Wow!

And the good news just kept coming. A week or two after that, the staff at Cardinal Hill told me they felt I was ready to go home. I left on a weekend at the end of April. They told me they wanted to see me again in the summer for a month to work on some more advanced wheelchair skills. I had no problem with that at all. I was so excited to have learned all that I did: the wheelchair maneuvers, showering, getting on and off my bed.

The therapy was extremely intense. It required many hours and started out pretty rough, but it was worth every minute in the end. I'd gone from lying paralyzed on the school floor wondering if I were going to live, to feeling more alive than at any point in the last four-plus months. Cardinal Hill, as I learned, wasn't just about physical recovery, but mental recovery. Talking about my condition every day, whether to a television station or to the friends I made there, was very therapeutic.

I was so grateful for all that the staff at Cardinal Hill, the staff at Lourdes, my family and my friends had done for me. And I was proud of me for putting my trust in the Lord, working hard and refusing to give up. I felt I deserved to go home and couldn't wait to get there.

We pulled into the driveway to find a huge welcome-home party waiting for me. How huge? There were so many people there that they spilled into the yard. Radio stations were giving out our address over the airwaves.

Some people I knew. Some I didn't. There were a lot of kids from school, a big banner that said, "Welcome Home Missy," tons of balloons and people cheering and yelling for me. There was even one boy there who had been a friend of Michael's. He always wore black, shaved his fingernails to a sharp point, and oftentimes wore a dark trench coat. He seemed so strange to me when we were in school, yet he was one of the first people to give me a hug at my party. It shocked me and was a good example that we can't judge a book by its cover. It was amazing how much love there was and how the tragic shooting brought friends and strangers of all walks of life together. It was much like receiving all of the cards, letters, and gifts I had received at Lourdes, but on a smaller and more personal scale. To see people I'd never met in and around my house all because of their concern for me was surreal, and that love spilled over into Heath where I would start school again about a week later.

Dad drove us to school in our new van, generously donated by Stevens Chevrolet in Ballard County. There were just a couple weeks of school left and not a whole lot of catching up I could do in that short period of time, but the point of going was more to get acclimated to going back and seeing all my friends. When we pulled up, Dad offered to go in with Mandy and me, but we didn't want him to. We felt strong enough to enter the school on our own. He'd never walked us in before, and there was no need to start then.

Mr. Bond was out front to greet us. I wheeled in through the same double doors at the front of the school that I'd walked through six months earlier, the ones at the front of the lobby. There were banners everywhere welcoming me back. Students had decorated my locker. I got hugs every direction I turned, including a big one from Mrs. Beckman, the teacher who had been kneeling at my side and praying with me after I was shot.

As soon as the hugs were finished, the prayer circle began. I wheeled my way to the exact spot where I had been standing just before Michael began shooting. The prayer circle was amazingly different this time, though, for one reason: it was bigger than it had ever been. It seemed like every kid in the school was in it. Even Michael's friends who used to stand outside it by the trophy case were now a part of it. The hugs and banners were great, but nothing topped the solidarity and power of the circle that morning.

When it was over and the students started heading for class, I asked Mandy to stay back and recount what happened the morning of the shooting. I wanted her to show me where I was lying after I was shot. I don't know why I had her do that other than I just wanted to know if my memory of it all was correct – and it was. I wasn't bothered at all by being there. There were no tears. No nervousness. The lobby looked the same way it always did.

Perhaps I was so calm partly because the other students went about their business and acted as if they were long past that day. Because of their demeanors, I didn't see any reason for me to be upset about it. The students were great: my support group, one could say. I never had to see a psychologist. My friends were my therapists. Many people thought I might never come back to Heath, but what would be the point of that? What Michael did could happen at any school. I wasn't going to be scared. This was my school and would be from where I would graduate with all of my friends.

When it came time to go to classes, Mandy and I honestly did very little. We learned what we could but, having missed the majority of the school year, that effort was pretty futile. We didn't even have to take final exams. I don't think we had any right advancing to our junior year, but they passed us anyway. After what had happened, I'm sure it never even crossed the minds of teachers and administrators to fail us and leave us behind our friends. We'd just have to work extra hard our junior year, and that was fine with us.

As nice as it was to go back, school also posed many challenges, the biggest being the bathroom issue. I was pleasantly surprised to find that Mr. Bond had made one of my biggest concerns about it go away: the privacy issue. He had designated one bathroom in the school as my bathroom, even giving me my own key for it. But I was still getting to know how my body worked since the shooting, and I didn't always cath when I was supposed to do so.

My second or third day back at Heath, I realized just before lunch that I had wet myself. Fortunately I saw it before anybody else had noticed, but it was still so humiliating. I went to the office and cried. A couple people asked if I was alright, and I just told them I'd be fine. There were two girls I knew who happened to be in the office at that time whom I told: one was a friend from my days with her as a Girl Scout, and the other was Taylor. It felt good to tell them rather than trying to hide it because I knew they'd be mature about it and would keep it confidential.

Dad came to pick me up and we went home. A few days later when I wet myself again, I just changed my clothes and went back to class. Wetting myself that first time was emotionally rough. The second time I realized that it was part of who I was and always would be, and I couldn't go home every time it happened.

The school year was finished at the end of May, and looking back on it was kind of surreal. I had been on a typical teenage path at the start of the year where my biggest concerns were my friends, boys, clothes, and looks. But God severely altered my course. Why? I had no idea at the time, but I felt I would eventually figure it out.

Summer vacation had arrived and it would be an interesting one, to say the least. It started with a rigorous camp where I participated in several scary activities that I would have never thought I could have done if I hadn't tried. And I got a little more than I bargained for there when I was hit by a car – driven by Mandy! I did some more advanced rehabilitation at Cardinal Hill and saw a huge addition put on our house, thanks to the good people of Paducah, and, of course, attended that awesome Backstreet Boys concert! I followed that up in August with the start of my junior year at Heath and, in December, faced Michael for the first time since the day he shot me.

Considering six months earlier I was lying on a gurney in an emergency room with two bullet holes in my body, I felt I was going into summer vacation on a pretty high note, having come back significantly physically and mentally. I'd experienced plenty of obstacles along the way, and there would be plenty more to come. I just needed to keep my optimism and continue working hard toward leading a normal life in a wheelchair. I would prove to myself during the summer just how capable I was of doing that, and how I could do so much more than I ever imagined.

10

NO RISK, NO GAIN

I was at the mall in Paducah one day in May 1998 when I was approached by a man I had never met before. He recognized me because of all the publicity I had received since the shooting, and he had an idea of something I could do that might help me. This was becoming a common occurrence: people offering help or advice or just saying hi, knowing who I was without me knowing who they were. It seemed rather strange and took some time to get used to, but it was also a blessing to meet so many people who cared about me.

He suggested that I look into attending the Shepherd Center's annual "Adventure Skills Workshop" at the end of the month. The Shepherd Center, based in Atlanta, was a hospital that cared for and rehabilitated people with catastrophic injuries, including spinal cord injuries.[23] They held the one-week workshop in southern Alabama where I could try everything from water skiing to scuba diving. He thought it might be something I would like, and I agreed. It sounded risky but also sounded like a lot of fun and would be a good test of my courage and abilities since the shooting.

Two days after school let out for the year I was off to
the camp. Mom, Dad, Aunt Sissy, and Uncle Dale went
along and stayed in a hotel. Christie and Mandy also
attended the camp with me. Though I'd gotten some
great training at Cardinal Hill on how to live in a
wheelchair, I was still fairly new at it and wasn't comfortable enough being on my own. Everyone at the
camp was in a wheelchair and several had family members or friends there to help them, so I wasn't the only
one with that security.

We slept in huge cabins, all the girls in one and all
the boys in another. Unlike the tough regimen I was on
at Cardinal Hill, the camp was much more relaxing. I
woke up when I wanted to wake up, ate breakfast when
I wanted to eat, and participated in whatever activities I
was comfortable. But I added a twist to the trip: the
Today Show on NBC asked if they could tag along and
videotape my experience. I had no problem with that at
all. I figured having them there was a good way to
document my experience. But it turned out something
else good came from their presence: I felt obligated to
try just about every activity, no matter how scared I was.

Who knew that I could water ski? Not I, not even
before the shooting. I was scared to death and would
have backed out in a heartbeat if the *Today Show* weren't
taping. I didn't even learn how to swim until I was in
fifth grade and never did become a very good swimmer.
I also didn't like being strapped to the board they placed
me on and was kind of creeped out by what creatures
might be out there in the water. It was a far cry from
anything I'd ever done in Paducah, but I did it. They
strapped me on, attached it with a rope to the back of the
boat, and off I went! But that was just the beginning.

I also rode a Jet Ski, paddled a canoe, and did a little
scuba diving. I climbed a tree by getting strapped into a
harness, using my arms to pull myself up. I rode a horse,
which was a good test of my balancing ability. About

the only thing I didn't do was play basketball because it looked too rough. People were banging into each other pretty hard and getting knocked out of their chairs. I didn't see much point in doing that.

Participating in all of those other activities, though, helped my confidence immensely. What was ironic was that I tried more new things in a wheelchair that week than I had tried my entire life before the shooting. I'd never ridden a Jet Ski or gone scuba diving, nor would I probably ever have done any of that had I not been paralyzed. The camp brought so much out of me that I never knew I had: the courage to take risks, the willingness to try new things, and the confidence that I could do anything.

The only downside to my new attitude was that I may have been a little overzealous one day when I decided to try something not on the camp's agenda. It was something Mandy would also try that would result in my second close call with death in six months.

A group of us took a break from the activities for a few minutes one day and hung out near the camp's parking lot. In the group were Mandy, Christie, me, a guy who was attending the camp as support for someone else and had a personal video camera, and a paraplegic girl who owned an absolutely gorgeous black Toyota Celica convertible. The *Today Show* crew was off somewhere else, and it was a good thing considering what we did.

Mandy and I had just gotten our learning permits to drive the previous week. We'd never driven before, but figured what better time to try it out than at the camp where I had tried so many new things already.

The girl with the Celica offered to let me get behind the wheel of her car and give it a test drive down the camp's long driveway while she rode in the passenger seat and Mandy rode in the back. The car was equipped with hand controls for a paraplegic. Both the gas and brake were to the left of the steering wheel. With some rods and wires, they were connected to the gas pedal and brake on the floor.

With Christie's and Mandy's help, I got behind the wheel and was so excited. Had the shooting not happened, I probably would have gotten my permanent license about this time, so I was more than ready to give it a try. The guy with the video camera taped this historic event for me while Christie sat in the nearby grass and watched. I'll admit that I was scared when I started to go, but the ride wasn't more than a couple hundred feet and I wasn't going very fast. The sense of freedom I felt was unbelievable. I did pretty well, keeping the car at a slow, steady speed and on the road. It was another feather in my cap of new things I had tried and was successful at during the camp. In fact, I made it look so easy that Mandy decided to give it a whirl. Even though there were hand controls, the car could still be driven using the gas pedal and brake on the floor. That's what Mandy chose to do since that's how she would eventually learn to drive.

So I went back in my wheelchair on the grass next to Christie while Mandy jumped in the front seat and behind the wheel. Her first test was to flip the car in reverse and turn it around so she could head back up the driveway. She did that pretty well, but when she shifted the car from reverse to drive and began to move forward up the driveway, she struggled to hit the brake. The pole that ran from the hand control to the brake was in her way. In a panic, she reached for the hand control but shifted it in the wrong direction! She ended up giving the car more gas and was losing control of where she was going. And guess where she was headed? Right toward Christie and me!

The car didn't seem like it was going that fast, but it was fast enough and close enough that I froze like a deer in headlights. I sat there staring powerlessly as it rumbled toward me. I screamed at Mandy and the girl to stop. Christie jumped up and tried to pull me out of the way, but we had put the brakes on the chair when I had gotten back in it after driving. We couldn't get the wheels unlocked fast enough. It was a horrible, helpless feeling. There was nothing Christie or I could do, and Mandy still hadn't figured out how to stop the car.

As I realized what was about to happen to me, a million thoughts ran through my head: Am I seriously about to be hit by a car just six months after being shot? How many people have been shot and hit by a car in their lives? How do I explain this to the camp directors and my parents? What will the newspaper headlines read? How about, "Girl in wheelchair run over by twin sister," or simply, "Are you kidding me?"

The car struck me and the chair hard enough and low enough that I was tossed into the air and onto the hood. I then slid off and tumbled hard to the ground, a few feet in front of one of the moving tires. I lay there unable to move, watching the wheel roll toward me. Fortunately for all of us, Mandy finally found the hand brake – and just in time. The car came to a halt with the front right tire stopping just inches from my body.

Mandy jumped out of the car, crying hysterically, but luckily the damage was minimal. The car made it through unscathed. The wheelchair survived the hit. As for me, I suffered a scraped elbow and a broken fingernail. The fellow with the video camera – yes, he taped the whole incident – happened to be an emergency medical technician. The biggest concern was that I could have been injured anywhere below my chest and not have known it because of my inability to feel anything, even pain, but he checked me out and said I was fine.

We went back to our cabins and agreed that as long as we were at camp, that incident never happened. We even rewound the tape that night and recorded over the evidence. We didn't want the camp or us to get in any trouble. We finally did tell our parents the following week when we took a little side vacation to Panama City, Florida. Surprisingly they weren't upset, probably because it had been a week since it happened and Mandy and I were actually laughing about the whole incident by then. But Mandy did take some ribbing for a long time from family and friends for her driving skills.

Overall, the camp was an awesome experience, driving and all. It was a time I'll never forget because I learned how to do things I never imagined I could do. My confidence level was sky high, and it was a great way to start my summer vacation. We left Alabama when the camp was over and headed to Florida for a few days on the beach before finally going home.

Before the shooting I had been part of the dating scene in high school. I had a couple boyfriends in 1997 and was ready to start dating again after getting home from Florida, or so I thought. I went out with one guy that summer of 1998, but he broke up with me because he said he was tired of dating Mandy and me. What did he mean by that? Well, every time we had gone out on a date, I took Mandy with me. I think his friends were giving him a hard time about "dating" both of us and he'd finally had enough. But I couldn't promise not to bring Mandy anymore. That's because Mandy knew what I had to do when it came to going to the bathroom.

Now I know what I have to do when it comes to cathing. Every five hours I need to do it. It's that simple. And I can do it pretty quickly. But back then I was still learning how my body worked, how to do the cathing and trying to figure out how often I needed to do it. I was just 16 years old. There was no way I was going to explain cathing to a boy I liked. It was way too embarrassing. I just wasn't ready to talk about it.

I also had the problem of wondering whether boys who wanted to go out with me were interested in me, Missy Jenkins, or were just captivated at the thought of going out with that well-known girl who was shot at Heath. There were many advantages to being as publicly recognized as I was, but dating was not one of them.

A good example was a guy I had met at our local bowling alley that summer. He was really cute, and we swapped phone numbers before we went our separate ways that night. We ended up calling each other and hung out a few times at my house. I really thought there was a spark there until he invited me over to his house to meet his parents. The whole time I was there I felt like I was being interviewed by them. I didn't mind the questions, but it went on all night. When the night was over, he didn't want anything to do with me anymore. I don't know why, but maybe it's because he realized after that "interview" that the only reason he liked me was because I was that girl who was shot, not because of who I really was.

I finally decided that maybe I just wasn't ready to date yet. I wanted to, but I didn't see how it could work, at least not yet. What was the point in going out with someone I liked when I knew I wouldn't be ready to tell him about everything I had to go through? All that would result in it for me would be a broken heart. Why put myself through that? I needed to focus on myself and believe that problem would be solved in time with maturity. The more I learned about me and my body and how to manage every aspect of my life as a paraplegic, the easier things like dating would become, and the easier it would be to find that right guy. I guess it was no different than anything else since the shooting – it would take time to get back on track.

I focused on myself in July when I went back to Cardinal Hill for about a month to learn some advanced wheelchair skills. It was much of the same as far as the setup: a strict schedule, no family allowed to stay with me, but I was prepared for it that time around. I did some strenuous exercises and weight training before learning how to get from the floor into a wheelchair; up steps and curbs; dressed while in my wheelchair; and in and out of a car.

The summer also included that fantastic Backstreet Boys concert with the backstage passes. Mandy and Christie went with me, and I was so excited to go. To that point, aside from some of the news reporters who interviewed me, I hadn't met anybody famous yet, so I was pretty starstruck. We were able to go backstage before the concert and meet the whole band: Kevin Richardson (whose brother obtained the passes and tickets for us), Nick Carter, Howie Dorough, Brian Littrell and A.J. McLean. Nick was my favorite. When he walked into the room, the whole place went silent. Mandy went up to Nick and asked him for a hug. He obliged, so I said "Hey, she's my twin sister. You can't hug her without hugging me!" So he did. It was a great time and awesome concert, which we were honored to watch from the front row.

I realize that had I not been a victim in the shooting, I never would have had many opportunities like that, and it felt good to get that special treatment. It made me feel that what happened to me wasn't all that bad and that people really cared about me. I felt lucky to get opportunities like that and was very gracious to the people who made them happen. Yes, I did feel guilty about it at times. If I had become a paraplegic in another way, as many people do, I wouldn't have had the opportunities I was given.

Look at all the people I was with at the camp and at Cardinal Hill. They were in the same situation or worse than I was, yet they didn't get half of the public attention I was receiving. I wasn't just a girl in a wheelchair to people. I was that girl shot in that school in that prayer circle by that teenage boy. I was a celebrity in a strange sense, not because of anything I had accomplished, but because of what happened to me and the big deal that the public made out of it. But I learned to live with the attention. I thought, "You know, this is what God wanted for me. This is what He wanted my life to be like. I need to enjoy it and create as much good from it as I can." I guess God knew I could do that, and I felt lucky that He picked me to fill that role in the world. Maybe I was starting to figure out why He let this happen to me. He knew I had the character and ability to turn it into something positive for the world to see.

The summer concluded with the start of an addition put on to the back of our house, completely free of charge. All of the materials and labor were supplied by people of Paducah, some whom we knew and others who were total strangers. They added an enormous section that included a living room, dining room, and kitchen. To the back of that room they added a bathroom and bedroom for me. Our house that seemed smaller with the addition of Mom's wheelchair and my wheelchair practically doubled in size. It was completed by the spring of the following year.

While the whole shooting experience cast a negative light on our community, the addition to the house was a great example of just how many good people we had in Paducah. Michael and his actions got most of the attention. My plight was also in the spotlight on a regular basis. But there was so much good that came from what happened that fateful day, with the dozens of people building and paying for that addition being just one example. It was so awesome watching them do it. It was amazing how everybody was unconditionally willing to take care of us in our time of need.

My junior year at Heath started in August, and I was excited to get back for my first full school year since my freshman year. It was a little odd when I got there because new security measures were everywhere. We had a chain-link fence around the school, a police officer in the building, cameras mounted throughout the school, and we all had to wear identification badges. It felt like overkill, but aside from the badges being annoying hanging from a lanyard around our necks all day, we all knew it was for good reason.

My only concern was that many of these measures seemed to be in place to stop people on the outside from getting in. Michael wasn't an outsider and wouldn't have been stopped from getting in by a fence, badge, camera, or officer. But as the years would go on and more and more shootings would occur at the hands of outsiders (such as two in 2006: one in Bailey, Colorado, in which a man walked into a school and killed a girl,[24] and one in Lancaster County, Pennsylvania, in which a gunman killed five children in a one-room Amish school[25]), sadly we would see that protecting our buildings from the outside was just as important.

My school days were pretty normal, aside from the fact that I had physical therapy there. I went into an empty classroom with a therapist from a physical therapy center in Paducah during my lunch break three times a week. I lay on the floor while he or she stretched my legs and monitored me as I lifted weights. I did this each time for about 30 minutes. My friends would sometimes hang out in the room with me, using their time constructively – by playing in my wheelchair!

I was back to doing many of the things I had started to do my sophomore year. I was in the marching band again. I had to sit in my wheelchair on the sidelines during the football games and play, but the director set up the routines so that some of them connected to me during the performances, which was pretty neat. It was actually kind of nice because during competitions I didn't have to be judged on our marching starts or stops. If we messed up, I knew it wasn't me! The only difficult part was that because I was off to the side, I couldn't hear the other flutists playing. That sometimes made it difficult to stay in sync, but I got better at it the more we did it.

I was also in the choir, was elected president again of the FHA since I didn't get to serve my term the previous year, and became part of a support group with my friends.

The group was something we wanted to form and was encouraged by our school counselor, Alan Warford. He sat in on our weekly meetings, but we were the ones who did most of the talking. We all had done a great job of putting the shooting behind us and looking toward the future, but we also knew that what happened that day was never going to leave our minds. Some of us had been hurt physically. All of us had been hurt mentally. I'd never seen a therapist about it. Mandy did for a little while, but said it didn't do her a whole lot of good. The support group, however, did help her, probably because everyone in the group was there that tragic day.

The meetings were informal and there was really no set agenda going into each one. We just got together and talked about how we each coped with the terrible memories. For some, it was visiting the graves of Jessica, Kayce, and Nicole. For others, it was strictly through prayer. Some even tried to laugh about it, not because of a lack of respect for those who were killed or those of us who were injured, but because sometimes humor is the only way some people know how to get through a difficult situation. We met for a little more than three months. It was obvious that with each meeting we became more comfortable with ourselves and with what we were dealing with. The meetings also helped prepare us for what was coming up in mid-December: Michael's sentencing.

I hadn't paid any attention to what was going on with Michael since the day he'd been arrested. I really didn't care. I knew what he'd done, and I knew he was in jail. I was reminded every day of what he did to me when I tried to get out of bed, get dressed, or go to the bathroom. I didn't need to dwell on him. My focus was on me. But I did hear that he had decided to plead guilty due to mental illness.

Was he mentally ill that day? Some doctors said he was. Others said he wasn't. If he was, I never noticed it. But by entering the plea he did, the families of those who died and the rest of us didn't have to testify and go through a trial. We were, however, given the chance to speak to Michael face to face and tell him whatever we wanted. And those of us in the support group found out that was ultimately all that we needed.

On December 16, 1998, Michael was sentenced. The judge allowed me and several others to address him in court before they took him away, and we didn't hold back our feelings. After that, we never had another support group meeting again. We didn't need to.

11

THE SENTENCING

Two days after the shooting, McCracken County Sheriff Frank Augustus said he believed Michael may not have been the only person involved in planning the attack.[26] While Michael claimed during his interrogation just two hours after the shooting that he acted alone, the sheriff's doubt appeared to be for good reason. Consider the fact that Michael brought several guns with him and had thousands of shotgun shells in his backpack. During another interrogation on December 4, just three days after the shooting, Michael claimed he and four other students had talked about taking over their school two years earlier.

"Well, we came up with the main idea probably about seventh grade," Michael told Detective Carl Baker with the McCracken County Sheriff's Department and Lt. Dean Hayes with the Kentucky State Police. "But I mean, it was just like, we talked about it every now and then."

Baker then asked Michael if all four kids agreed to help him if enough guns were there.

"Yeah, but they didn't think that we were serious about it," Michael said.

"How do you know they didn't," Baker asked. "You were serious about it. What makes you think that they didn't think you were serious?"

"Uh, I, I don't believe that anyone thought that any of us were serious," Michael replied. "Everybody just thought that it was just something to talk about."[27]

So what's my take on it? I think at some point Michael probably did talk to his friends about taking over their school, and they may have talked about it with him, but he's the only one who, at least on the day of the shooting, took it as a reality.

There are times kids talk and joke about things but don't really mean what they say and don't intend to act on them. That's why some other students (aside from those four boys) who were told by Michael that something big was going to happen on that day didn't say anything to anybody. Nobody back then, at Heath or anywhere else, took such threats seriously.

One of those kids Michael told was a boy I grew up with who went to Heath and was one of my best friends. He was in the gym at a basketball meeting when the shots were fired. When Mandy and Taylor ran into the gym, Mandy told him what had happened. He immediately got upset and told Mandy that Michael had told him the week before that "something big" was going to happen that day, but he said Michael hadn't specifically said what it would be.

Several years later, when he and I were both in college, he called me on the phone out of the blue. He was crying. He said that he felt like what happened to me that day was his fault. He said he should be the one in the wheelchair instead of me because he should have told somebody what Michael told him. That wasn't the first time he'd expressed his guilt to me about that. I don't know what triggered him to call me that night, but he was more upset than anytime previously. I assume maybe he had been talking about the shooting with someone, and it brought back all the guilt he'd felt for so long.

But I told him that night what I had told him for years: it absolutely, positively was not his fault. No way, no how. It wasn't his fault, or the fault of anyone else to whom Michael may have said the same thing. People who may not agree need to realize a few things.

First of all, as previously mentioned, Michael was the class clown. He was always joking around, always saying things to get attention or to make people laugh. Nobody ever took him seriously about anything. That situation with my friend was no different. What Michael said to him could have meant anything, or nothing at all. "Something big" could have meant he was going to start a food fight in the cafeteria or play a prank on someone. But bring guns to school and kill people? There is no way in the world my friend could have known Michael was going to do that. There is no way anyone could have expected my friend to even conceive that notion.

Secondly, people need to understand that this was 1997. The 1999 shooting at Columbine High School in Littleton, Colorado that left 15 dead hadn't even happened yet. The 2007 shooting at Virginia Tech University that left 33 dead[28] was 10 years in the future. School shootings were extremely rare. The shooting at our school, along with the one in Pearl, Mississippi, just two months earlier were the first two school shootings in our nation's history to get the kind of extensive media attention that they got.

We weren't taught then, as kids are today, to not make jokes about "something big" happening. We weren't taught then, as kids are today, to tell someone in authority anytime a threat was made, no matter how false the claim may have been. We didn't have a school resource officer. We didn't have security cameras. We didn't have a fence around our school. We didn't have rules on the types of backpacks we could bring in or what could be in those backpacks. Weapons on school grounds were never an issue. A gun in a school? C'mon. Heck, we didn't even have locks on our lockers, and not once did I ever have anything stolen out of mine. How many public schools today can make that claim? That's how close and trusting we all were of each other.

The fact is that one big reason for all the security measures in schools nationwide today, and one reason why kids are taught to take everything so seriously, is because of what happened in our school that day. We were the example. People learned from us, but we had nobody to learn from ourselves.

So for my friend to say he should have told someone is simply unrealistic. If that threat were made today, then yes, someone should know to tell, but back then nobody would have even considered it. I can say, without a doubt, that if Michael had told me something was going to happen, I wouldn't have done anything about it. And most likely nobody who was at Heath that day could honestly say they would have done anything either.

Did some students at school pick on Michael? Yes. Did he tell some students that "something big" was going to happen? Yes. But that shouldn't skew people into thinking that the shooting was anybody's fault but his. He was the only one who knew what he was going to do that day. He chose to walk into school and kill Jessica, Kayce, and Nicole. He chose to shoot and injure five of us. Nobody made him do it. It was all of his own volition. He, and only he, was responsible for ruining the lives he ruined, for taking away the comfort and peace of our school and town.

Michael's actions that day prompted the families of the girls who were killed to file a multimillion-dollar lawsuit. They sued dozens of people and entities: Michael, his parents, teachers, school administrators, students, video game makers, movie makers, and Web sites all in an effort, they said, to get as many answers as possible about what happened. In the end, judges dismissed their claims against everyone but Michael. The families agreed on a $42 million settlement with his attorneys, though I don't think they have ever collected any of it, or ever will.[29]

The families asked my family to join them in their suit against all of those people and companies, but we didn't do it. I talked it over with my parents, and I ultimately decided that we weren't going to participate. I understood the anger those families felt. I understood their need for answers and their desire to hold people accountable for their actions or inactions. But I just couldn't blame anybody except Michael for what happened. He planned it. He pulled the trigger. It was, in my opinion, nobody's fault but his.

Michael pleaded "guilty but mentally ill" on October 5, 1998, to three counts of murder, five counts of attempted murder and one count of first-degree burglary (the burglary was for the guns and ammunition he stole from his friend's house the week before, as he talked about when he was interrogated hours after the shooting).[30] But was he really mentally ill?

He underwent three psychiatric and psychological evaluations by three different doctors that summer at the request of Tim Kaltenbach, the commonwealth's attorney who prosecuted the case.[31] During those evaluations Michael described the shooting and events leading up to it, from the bullying he faced in school to everything he did to acquire the guns and ammunition. Michael was asked by one psychologist if he thought what he did was caused by a mental disorder or mental illness.

"I don't think there's anything wrong with me," Michael said. "There may be, but if there is, that may be a reason, but if there's nothing really wrong with my head, there's no reason."[32]

The doctors said in their evaluation, "There were no indications that Michael Carneal suffers from any current psychotic symptoms or had ever done so in the past."[33]

After their evaluations, all three doctors signed off on the following conclusion: "It is our professional opinion that Michael Carneal was not mentally ill nor mentally retarded at the time of the shootings. It is our professional opinion, to a reasonable degree of medical probability, that Michael Carneal did not meet the criteria to be considered legally insane, or not criminally responsible."[34]

But Michael was also evaluated by a psychologist and psychiatrist at the request of his defense attorneys, Chuck Granner and Thomas Osborne.[35] The psychologist said, "Michael did report a number of paranoid fears which are abnormal and symptomatic of disturbed thinking." He reported that Michael said he feared "someone might be hiding under his bed or in his closet," and he feared going out at night. He also said Michael feared that "someone might spy on him through the heating vent in the bathroom floor."[36] The psychologist said Michael's symptoms were most consistent with a condition known as Schizotypal Personality Disorder, which is "characterized by features often seen in Schizophrenia, but without the severe deterioration into psychosis."[37] He concluded that while Michael "did not lack the capacity to control his conduct and refrain from committing the crime," he suffered "from mental disorders which rendered him seriously emotionally disturbed or mentally ill at the time of the offense."[38]

The psychiatrist came to similar conclusions. She said:

> "Although Michael knew right from wrong and had some capacity to control himself, this capacity was likely diminished by virtue of mental illness."[39]

I can't say for sure what Michael's mental condition was the day of the shooting. I didn't see him or talk to him that day. But I do know that I never saw signs previously that he was mentally ill, including the week before at that party we both attended. If he was mentally ill, he hid it well.

He was sentenced on December 16, 1998, in McCracken County Circuit Court.[40] But in the minutes before that, nine of us were given the opportunity to tell him what our thoughts and emotions were about his actions. Judge Jeff Hines said it was unusual to give that many people the opportunity to speak to an offender, but the whole case was unusual. I think Judge Hines felt it was the least he could do for us since nothing – not even sending Michael away for life – was going to fully heal the wounds.

The sentencing began at 4 P.M. Michael was dressed in tan pants and a long-sleeved, light-blue shirt. He walked into the courtroom in handcuffs, sat down in a chair next to his attorney, and put his head down. The first to speak was Kayce's mom, Sabrina Steger, who talked for about eight minutes. She cried at times but was able to keep her composure throughout. She told Michael how his actions had thrown her family's everyday lives into turmoil.

> "Dinner is usually sitting in the family room. The empty chair at the dining room table is too painful of a reminder. Even answering the simple question of how many children do you have has become very complicated," she said. "Knowing that we will not hear Kayce's voice, be able to kiss her goodnight or watch her graduate from high school is something that we live with constantly. How do we accept that someone intentionally took our daughter's life? There is no word in our language that comes close to describing the pain of losing a child.
>
> "Kayce's death will continue to affect our family in ways that only others who have lost children can

understand. Before December 1, our children were thriving. Now they just survive – and one couldn't even do that."

Mrs. Steger was followed by Kayce's father, Wayne Steger, who spoke succinctly for about 90 seconds. He said he saw Kayce off to school that morning and that she told him not to forget to pick her up. Her last words, he said, were "Dad, I love you."

"I find it very difficult to put into words what happened to us," Mr. Steger said as he began to cry. "Kayce did not have a second chance. She took a bullet to the back of the head and she was dead before she hit the floor."

He asked the judge to make sure that Michael did not "have a second chance."

The Steger's were followed by Nicole's parents, Chuck and Gwen Hadley. Mr. Hadley spoke for about a minute and Mrs. Hadley about two minutes. Mr. Hadley mentioned Nicole's dreams of attending the University of North Carolina with a friend and becoming a doctor, dreams she would never recognize.

"We don't know why this happened," he said. "We may not ever, ever know."

Mrs. Hadley cried as she spoke. She talked about her bout with depression after the shooting.

"As a mother, my life has forever been changed. My family is not whole anymore. When Michael Carneal murdered my daughter, Nicole, he also did a lot of damage to my family. My heart's been torn apart and it's not ever going to heal – there's always going to be a hole in it.

"When I go to sleep at night, I don't sleep at night," she continued. "When I close my eyes, I see my beautiful Nicole with her face marred with a bullet hole in her head. I see her thick, beautiful hair matted with her own blood, and I see her lying in a casket. Parents aren't supposed to bury their children, but I've had to do that."

Jessica's dad, Joe James, spoke next for about seven minutes. He was very critical of Michael, and, in the opinion of many, rightfully so.

"My Jessica no longer lives here and it was not by any choice she or her parents made. It was by a choice that was made by a 14-year-old spoiled brat," he said. "The shooter has killed not only my daughter, but has killed a part of my being as well."

He said that someone had made the comment that Michael's parents had suffered more than anyone else in the county.

"C'mon, give us a break," he said. "John and Ann still have a son and will be able to shower him with gifts and affections for several years to come, and I get to clean and polish a marker in the cemetery."

Kelly Hard was next. If Mr. James' speech wasn't scathing enough, Kelly took care of that during the next four minutes. She cried hard, at times struggling to keep her composure, but her words were very direct and powerful. The following is the entire text of what she said. Considering the fact that she was one of the people Michael shot, I think it's worth printing in its entirety to give you a sense of the depth of her anger and how much his actions affected her:

"I haven't really made up anything to say, but I'm mainly speaking to Michael because this is what I've wanted since the whole thing happened. I don't understand. I don't care what excuses you gave. I don't care how you feel. All I know is what I saw that day. I had to comfort my best friend's (Kayce's) family. I was the last one to see the girl I grew up with and was best friends with. I see that picture in my head every day and everything that you have done – EVERYTHING! And I don't care if you're sorry. You should have thought of

that before you even did it. You should have thought of
it.

"In my eyes – I know that people will put me down
for this – but I would love to see you get the death
penalty. I know you can't get it, but you gave them the
death penalty and they didn't do anything for it. You
did. They didn't choose. In my eyes you chose – you
chose the death penalty. You chose to do this. They did
not choose to live with that. You chose. In my eyes, you
chose death. I'm not wounded as bad as Missy, which is
my other best friend, and I have to comfort her and be
with her every day and I love her and I hate to see her
go through this. And it's all because of you being selfish
because you got called a few names which we didn't
call you. It's for nothing. I don't care if people called
you names. That does not justify killing somebody.
What is your value of life?

"I have my little scar. It's not much but it reminds
me every time I see it. It reminds me. And the pictures
in my head – I've had to go to psychiatrists and they
said I had conditions or whatever and it's all because of
you! I just want you to know that even though you're
not getting the death penalty or maybe not even getting
punished a whole lot at all, that no one will ever have
respect for you – and you obviously have no respect for
anyone else. And I hope you're suffering as much as we
are."

Stephen Keene, the brother of Craig Keene who was
shot, addressed Michael next for two minutes. He maintained an angry tone throughout.

"My statement is not specifically for this court. It is
for that young man sitting right there. Michael, I watched
you gun down three girls and murder them. I watched
you shoot my brother and try to kill him and five other
people. If I have to watch that – you look at me right
now."

Michael looked up at him, the first time he'd looked
up at anybody. Stephen continued.

"You know, I don't understand what your whole point is. What would drive somebody to do this man? Respond!" Michael continued to look at him, but said nothing. "I wish it was that easy," Stephen said. "I wish I couldn't respond to anything. I wish it was that easy for me."

When Stephen finished, Michael put his head back down.

Stephen was followed by Mandy. Her voice cracked throughout, but she maintained control and was very calm during her four-minute talk. She talked about how scared she is all the time and how easily she gets frustrated because of what he did to her mentally.

"I try my hardest to take care of Missy, but sometimes I just can't take it anymore. I feel selfish for feeling this way. It's not her fault. I'm not sure how I feel about Michael. I forgive him, but I am just upset with him. I know he needs help and I hope he gets it. I saw him on the news the other day. All I did was cry when I saw him. The same feeling comes to me when I see pictures of Jessica, Kayce, and Nicole or when I hear the songs that were played at their funerals. I can't listen to them. I try my hardest to forget about everything."

The Carneal family is behind me as I prepared to speak to Michael during the sentencing on December 16, 1998. (Photo Dec. 17, 1998, *Paducah Sun*/Steve Nagy)

I was the last one to go. I kept it short – about 90 seconds. Like Mandy, I was very calm and fairly polite. I felt that if he was going to truly listen to what I had to say, there was a better chance of that happening if I spoke to him in a low, calm voice instead of yelling at him. Here is what I said, in its entirety:

"I just wrote down a couple things. I want Michael to look at me."

Michael looked at me and continued to look at me until I was finished talking.

"Alright – I want to tell you that I'm paralyzed. I'm paralyzed from my chest right here down. And I spent five months in the hospital, and I still struggle. And I feel really helpless. I can't do things like I used to. I can't do things on my own like I used to. I can't go to the bathroom like regular people. It's hard to get dressed. I see people running around doing stuff like everybody else, and I can't really do it because I'm stuck to my chair. They tell me that I'll never walk again. I think I will, though. But if God doesn't want me to walk, that's OK. And I just wanted you to know because I have to live with it everyday now.

"And I don't know why you did this to me and everybody else, but I know that I'm never going to forget it because I see it every day in my mind. But I don't have any hard feelings toward you. I'm just upset that this happened and I'm upset that everything had to go this way, but I can live this way. It's going to be hard, but I can do it. That's really all I had to say."

As I look back on my words that day, it's interesting to me how what I said to him still resonates today in my life: that I forgive him, that what he did to me is not going to keep me down and that I'm OK with whatever God's plan is for me. I think keeping on that course throughout my life after the shooting is a big reason why I've been able to not just survive that tragic day, but flourish in ways that I never imagined I could have as a paraplegic.

After I spoke, Judge Hines called Michael to stand before the bench. He sentenced him to 20 years in prison for the burglary and 20 years for each attempted murder count: a total of 120 years. That was trumped by the three concurrent life sentences without the possibility of parole for 25 years that Judge Hines gave him for the three murders, the maximum sentence Michael could have gotten. Judge Hines then spent a couple minutes addressing those of us in the courtroom:

"I wish there was something I could say that would do something. They think that sometimes you get a black robe and get elected to an office and you've got the answers. Well I can tell you, ladies and gentlemen, a year ago December the second, when I saw the biggest banner headline I've ever seen in my life on the *Paducah Sun* newspaper that said, 'Why?' I've been in this business for a long time. That's the one question that we frequently, most frequently, never get the answer to – no matter what. We never find the answer 'Why?' And that's the most fleeting thing for all of those of you who were affected by this physically, mentally and otherwise. I can't give you the answer. No way I could. Not going to try to. I don't know what it is – and I'll never know either."

He concluded by talking about how the night before, when he put his young daughter to bed, she asked him to hold her hand.

"The one thing that was flying through my brain last night was what it must be like to go in one of those rooms and hold that cold hand. I can't imagine the pain. I can't imagine. I really am sorry for everybody in this room. And God bless us – every one. That's the end of this sentencing."[41]

12

BULLYING

I mentioned earlier the psychiatrist hired by the defense who said that Michael knew right from wrong but had a diminished capacity to control himself because of mental illness. She also said the following:

"Years of being tormented in school and the failure of schools to intervene and remedy the situation contributed to his alienation, feelings of being ineffectual, his conviction that his peers did not care about him, and ultimately to his need to seek revenge."[42]

In other words, he was bullied. And she was right. Michael was the victim of constant bullying. No, I'm not going to make excuses for what he did to the eight of us that day. As I've said many times, what he did was his choice and nobody else's. He had plenty of nonviolent alternatives he could have chosen to deal with his problems. But I don't think there's any doubt that the never-ending bullying he endured was lingering in his mind as he planned his rampage and was a factor in his decision to do what he did.

What is bullying? To me, it's when somebody deliberately verbally, nonverbally or physically hurts someone else. Bullying has been around since the beginning of time but probably wasn't always called that, or even looked at as being a very serious issue. Until very late in the 20th century, bullying was perhaps considered by many people to be only physical. The verbal and nonverbal aspects of bullying have always been there but rarely acknowledged.

We can see when someone has been physically bullied. The proof is visibly there. But verbal and nonverbal forms of bullying attack the brain, emotions, and self-esteem of a person. They can be easily hidden by the recipient out of embarrassment, or overlooked by those around that person because they assume he or she will get over it. By verbal, I mean name-calling or insulting comments. By nonverbal, I mean ignoring people and making them feel alienated, acting as if they don't even exist. That, too, can crush a person's sense of worth and be emotionally traumatizing for him or her.

I can remember being verbally and nonverbally bullied growing up, and two of those times really stand out. One occasion I talked about briefly in the earlier chapter on forgiveness. Here are a few more details about that incident: I had just started the seventh grade at Heath Middle School. I had lost a ton of weight over the summer, dropping from a size sixteen to a size five, simply by eating better and exercising. I went to school feeling very good about myself. That is, until I got to English class on the first day. Some girls were standing together and talking before class when one of them, a girl I knew but not that well, turned away from the group, looked at me and said, "Missy, I have a question. Are you anorexic?" After asking the question, some of the girls in her group laughed.

In my mind, they were bullies as well for supporting her with their laughter. Everybody else in the room stood there and waited for me to give her an answer. Painfully embarrassed, I quietly said no, dropped my head, went over to my desk and sat down. How much did that affect me? Well, I still remember it vividly today, if that's any indication. If she really cared and wasn't trying to be a bully, she could have asked me that question privately.

What her question said to me was, "You used to be too fat, now you're too thin." In my mind, at that moment, I felt like there was no way I could win. I had done so much to better myself as a person and that was how I was greeted by my peers? I deserved better. Everybody deserves better.

The other time I recall being bullied was in third grade. There was a boy in my class who was one of my best friends. We used to help each other on assignments all the time. One day we got a paper back that I had helped him improve. He earned a really good grade and was so excited that he gave me a big hug right in front of everybody. That was the beginning of the end of our friendship. His friends laughed at him and teased him mercilessly. The next day, he wouldn't even acknowledge my presence. In fact, he never talked to me again.

To me, he was a bully for ignoring me and severing what had been a great friendship. The kids who teased him were also bullies to both of us. I realize we were only in third grade, but I think the old mantra of "sticks and stones will break my bones but names will never hurt me" is a bunch of garbage. People like to use that as an excuse, but the truth is that names do hurt. They can hurt much more than a punch in the face. A punch will sting for a while, maybe leave a bruise, but eventually it will go away. As you can see, something that hurt me emotionally two decades ago is still fresh in my mind today.

What also has hurt me mentally for years is the fact that I was a bully once myself when I was a kid. Mandy, Taylor, Eric, and I used to pick on a boy who lived down the street. We were older than he was and always thought he looked kind of nerdy. We called him names and just picked on him in general. It was all verbal abuse. I'm not proud to say that I was a part of that. The bullying hurt him. He'd always walk away dejected, sometimes crying, and we thought it was funny. We didn't care. And I don't know why we didn't care. Maybe part of it was that we were kids, and kids don't have much experience with empathy. Another part of it was that I was overweight at the time and was occasionally teased by people for being so big. I was insecure about myself, and very likely putting him down made me feel like I wasn't as bad as those who picked on me made me feel. I think that's a primary reason why a lot of people bully others – they don't want to face their own issues. Instead, they raise themselves up by putting others down.

Now imagine being the recipient of that bullying day after day after day. How would you feel? If you were treated that way every day at school, think of how tough it would be to get out of bed every morning, knowing that's what was awaiting you. Though none of us gave it much thought at the time, perhaps that's what Michael had to deal with.

Michael told that psychiatrist about several instances in which he was bullied in eighth grade at Heath Middle School and ninth grade at Heath High School. They included: being called a nerd and made fun of for the clothes and glasses he wore; being spit on frequently by a couple boys; a gossip column in the Heath Middle School newspaper that implied he was gay; being put through hazing rituals when he joined the high school band, such as having his head rubbed until it bled; having a science experiment ruined by another student on purpose, forcing him to do it over; and having his food stolen by a boy in the cafeteria, who then challenged Michael to a fight – and that boy's friends laughed at Michael when he backed down.[43]

I saw him get picked on. I also saw him tease others (remember when he ran around the room with a button that had a picture of Mandy and me, and he called us fat?). I could have stepped in and tried to stop others from picking on him or tried to stop him from picking on others, but back then it all just seemed like normal behavior for kids our age. Freshmen, especially, were picked on all the time. Aren't they in every high school?

Of course, now that I'm older, I realize how damning it was to Michael. That's why we need to make kids realize when they're very young what impact their actions and words can have on others for a lifetime. Acquaintances and I were guilty of bullying each other. We just didn't realize it as being a big deal while we were doing it. It's the same way with kids today, and that attitude needs to be changed.

So how do we fix the bullying problem? There's no simple answer, but there are some techniques that are worth trying. One is to teach children to ignore bullies. In many cases, bullies who don't get a reaction out of the person they're picking on will eventually get bored and stop. It's that reaction that makes them continue the teasing. Another method is to teach kids to tell someone in authority when they are being bullied or have witnessed bullying. I know to many that's called "tattling." But would you rather be known as a tattletale or be picked on to the point where you struggle to function in every day life?

Many states have also passed, or are trying to pass, legislation that would define bullying and require school districts to do something about it when it happens. That's probably a very good idea. If that's what it takes to make schools pay more attention to it, then it should be done.

But I think the best way to prevent bullying is to teach kids about it as soon as they start school. Make it part of the curriculum starting in kindergarten. Let kids role-play with each other in front of the class. Teach them what bullying is, how to recognize it, how to report it and how to stand up for each other. Bullying is not going to go away until kids are taught how to empathize – to put themselves in the shoes of a person being bullied. They need to be taught early, and they need to be taught often.

I was never taught about bullying and its effects. I wish I had been. I wish all the kids at Heath were. I wish Michael was. Maybe what Michael did to us wouldn't have happened if he hadn't been bullied. I have no idea. Nobody knows for sure. But knowing through his psychiatric evaluations how much the bullying seemed to bother him, it's enough reason for school personnel, parents, and students to take it seriously all the time, even if it means overreacting to situations every now and then. Until it is taken seriously all the time, it's not going to end. And as long as it doesn't end, people – innocent people – are going to get hurt.

13

COLUMBINE, CLINTON, AND CALIFORNIA

At the end of 1997 and throughout 1998, from just after the shooting until the sentencing, I'd received a great deal of media attention locally and nationally. It seemed like everybody wanted to know how I was doing, or what I had to say about bullying, guns, or school safety. But nothing compared to the attention I got in the first six months of 1999.

A week or two after the sentencing, I received a phone call from a representative with *Ladies Home Journal* magazine. The caller told me that I had been picked as one of the publication's most fascinating people of 1998 and wanted to know if I would accept the nomination and allow them to come to my house to do an interview for a television special. To get an idea of how big of a deal this was, take a look at the others who were on their list: Mary Hart, anchor of *Entertainment Tonight;* Mary Bono, California congresswoman and wife of the late singer Sonny Bono; Sarah Ferguson, Duchess of York; author Rebecca Wells; singers Trisha Yearwood and Queen Latifah; Judy Sheindlin of *Judge Judy* fame; and actresses Whoopi Goldberg, Drew Barrymore, and Camryn Manheim. And right smack in the middle of that list was a good old Kentucky girl named Missy Jenkins. Wow!

When I asked the representatives from the magazine "Why me?" they said that they viewed me as an heroic figure who beat the odds. They said I found a way to move on with my life despite the tragedy. They also liked the fact that I was out in the media talking about my experience, telling people what I had learned from it and how it made me a better person. I was so excited by the honor. Being on the list with those 10 well-known people made me feel very important and confirmed for me that what happened was about more than me being paralyzed. It was part of a much bigger plan that God had. It was about me accepting my disability and using it to become an inspiration for people around the world who were facing uphill battles. I was proof that with determination, effort, and the right attitude, anything was possible.

After that honor and Christmas break, I jumped right back into my daily routine at school for the second half of my junior year. I went for about a month before I took a couple days off in February to travel with Mandy to Chicago for an appearance on *The Oprah Winfrey Show*. We were so excited to go. Who wouldn't have been? Oprah was such a prominent and well-respected personality that we knew millions of people would watch us. I'd been on *Montel* the year before after the Jonesboro shooting, but that was by satellite. *Oprah* was my first appearance – and Mandy's, too – in front of a studio audience.

We were a little nervous about it. It wasn't like those times when people followed us around with cameras to tape us for future shows or news segments. If we messed up on *Oprah*, we couldn't just start over. Even though *Oprah* was taped and not shown live on television, there were no second takes because it was in front of a live audience.

But Oprah made Mandy and me feel comfortable, and we just pretended it was her and us in the room, as if the audience wasn't even there. It also went by very quickly, lasting maybe 10 or 15 minutes since she had other guests to interview.

What's interesting is my best memory of being on that show wasn't anything Mandy or I said, but the appearance of Mitchell Wright, who was a guest after us. He was the husband of teacher Shannon Wright who was killed in the Jonesboro shooting. It was such an honor to meet him and so sad at the same time.

Mitchell and Shannon had a two-year-old son. He talked about how he had to try to explain to his son that Mommy was never coming home. He also talked about what a wonderful teacher she was and how she was loved by her students. That made me think about our teachers at Heath and how fortunate we were to have them the day of the shooting. Our teachers did so much for us every day no matter what, but they outdid themselves that day acting as physicians and counselors. They were our angels, as I know Shannon is for her husband and son today.

Just two months later, on April 20, 1999, I was back on several news stations around the country after the deadliest high school shooting in the nation to that point occurred at Columbine High School. Twelve innocent students and a teacher were killed. Twenty-four others were wounded. The shooters were Eric Harris and Dylan Klebold, both students at the Littleton, Colorado, school who killed themselves after the massacre.[44]

I was hanging out after school making table decorations for our junior/senior prom coming up that weekend. We were in a classroom making little top hats to go with our theme "Party Like it's 1999," based on the song by Prince. We hadn't been working on them very long that afternoon when someone came running in and told us what was going on in Littleton. We turned on the television and heard the newscasters report that they didn't know how many were killed, but that there were likely several dead bodies in the school.

Once again, just like with Pearl and Paducah and Jonesboro, I was stunned. As they interviewed kids at Columbine, many of them talked about how the shots sounded like fireworks, which was exactly my thought when the shots rang out in our school lobby. But Columbine seemed to take school shootings to a whole different level. Not only were more students killed and injured, but it was torture for many of them who were held hostage or trying to take cover as Harris and Klebold ran rampant through the school. I couldn't imagine how terrifying that had to be for those students and teachers.

The shooting at our school could have been so much worse. Michael had enough guns and ammunition that he could have taken many more lives. Fortunately he stopped when he did. But at Columbine they just kept shooting.

Several members of the news media called me that day and the following days to get my reaction to what happened at Columbine. It always seemed a bit odd to me when someone would call and ask for my reaction to a tragedy such as that. Of course I was devastated and hurt. But after thinking about it, I realized they were just doing their jobs, and I took it as a compliment that they wanted my opinion. It became part of my purpose: to try to educate people on why it might have happened and how the healing could begin. Some were probably just looking for a sound bite, but others thought I could be helpful, so that's what I tried to do.

The media attention continued the following week at prom, and I didn't even know it. I went to the dance with an old friend who attended another school. It was kind of awkward because it was the first dance I'd gone to since I'd been in a wheelchair. When we got on the dance floor, we just looked at each other, unsure of what to do. Should he kneel down on the floor? Maybe sit on my lap? Pick me up and hold me? We finally decided I would sit and he would stand as we held hands and swayed. It was simple, and there was no chance of injuring ourselves.

Throughout the night there was a photographer at the dance taking pictures. I assumed he was hired by the school to take photos for the yearbook. But it seemed like wherever my date and I went, he went with us: on the dance floor, getting something to drink, hanging out at a table with friends. Other kids were looking at us kind of funny, wondering what was going on and why I was getting all of the attention. The photographer never said anything to us, and I never spoke to him. I figured he just wanted some extra photos of me because I was that girl who had been shot. But he was taking an exorbitant amount. Was this going to be the Missy Jenkins yearbook, I wondered? It wasn't until a couple weeks later that I found out what he was doing.

Before prom I had done an interview with *People* magazine. I talked about prom in that interview, and they asked me if they could come to it and shoot photos. I didn't want them to because I didn't want to be the center of attention that night. I just wanted to go and have fun with my friends. But somewhere along the way there must have been a miscommunication between *People* and me. It turns out that photographer was shooting photos for *People* and, sure enough, the photos ended up in the magazine alongside the story written from the interview. The story was good. The photos were nice. The photographer was professional and just doing his job. But it seemed to cause such a distraction at prom. Maybe it was my fault, but I vowed to never let that happen again. There was absolutely no way I would let something like that occur at the prom the following year – my senior year.

We ended up having a great time that night. Even dinner before the dance was fun, notwithstanding a slight problem. The restaurant we went to was not handicap accessible. It had two floors, and guess whose table was on the second floor? The workers there had to pick me up and carry me up and down the stairs! It was embarrassing, but I was able to laugh about it. A friend of mine had made the reservations and never gave the wheelchair issue a thought. She felt bad, but there was no reason to. It was something even I had a difficult time getting used to and still sometimes don't think about today when planning an activity. It was a small setback to an otherwise fun evening and fun conclusion to the school year.

I was proud of my comeback that year. Along with my band performances and serving as president of the FHA, I was also elected and served as vice president of the junior class. Before the shooting I would have never even considered running for office. I was way too shy. But the shooting encouraged me to try many new things. That, in turn, built up my confidence. I needed to do whatever I could whenever approached because those opportunities might never come again. I was given a second chance at life as a 15 year old and needed to take advantage of that – and I did.

On June 4, 1999, just weeks after my junior year concluded, I was given the opportunity of a lifetime. President Bill Clinton and First Lady Hillary Clinton were having a live discussion on *Good Morning America* from the White House about kids and guns, and I was asked to be a part of it!

I was flown to Washington, D.C., and was given a tour of the White House before the show started. Our discussion, which was facilitated by the show's hosts, Charles Gibson and Diane Sawyer, took place in the Roosevelt Room. I was in awe when the Clintons came in. It almost didn't seem real. I thought "Wow, they are sitting here right in front of me!"

There were probably about ten students involved in the discussion. Included were a boy named Albert from Illinois whose sister had been wounded by gunfire and a girl named Leeanne whose sister was killed in the Pearl shooting just two months before the Heath shooting.

The interview centered on the effects of guns on society and how kids can be influenced by what they see on television shows, in movies, and video games. We also talked about the use of metal detectors in schools, proposed gun legislation, and anonymous hot lines so kids could report the threat of violence.

I was quiet at the start of the program, still amazed and a little nervous at where I was and what was happening. But several minutes into the show, I finally found a comfortable point to jump in. I commented about video games and the effects on children. Michael had mentioned to investigators during his interrogation the day of the shooting that he had watched a movie called *Basketball Diaries* in which a boy dreamt of shooting people.[45]

> "I'm Missy Jenkins from Paducah and I've noticed, like, when I watch something like, that, something that's like with – you know, it doesn't affect me in any way. But there are some people that are a lot more sensitive. It makes it so much more of a reality to them that they kind of use that as a way to take care of their problems."[46]

OK, so I wasn't completely smooth in getting the words out, but not too bad! Hopefully people knew what I was trying to say. Considering I was 17 years old, on live national television and sitting in the President's house, I thought I did pretty well. But the best part was after the hosts followed what I said by mentioning that Japan has more violent video games and videos, yet only a handful of killings a year. That's when President Clinton jumped back into the conversation and said my name!

> "I want to make the point Missy did," he said. He continued by saying that while most kids in any culture will be OK, the average 18 year old in this country has seen 40,000 murders and 200,000 violent instances in the media, and that it's so much easier to get guns today than it used to be.
>
> "So if you have vulnerable kids, where the line between reality and fantasy blurs, they are more likely to be influenced by this," he said.[47]

How awesome was that! I thought, "Wow, the President just made a point by referring back to me!" It showed that he not only remembered my name but that he truly listened to what I said AND agreed with me AND it was important to him. It was a day I'll never forget.

My plan for the rest of the summer was to do some physical therapy and hang out with some friends, but that changed with an unexpected phone call at my home one day in June.

It was from a woman in Los Angeles with a company called Dynamics Walk Again Rehabilitation Center. She said Doctor Roy Douglas with the company had invented a brace that could help paraplegics walk. She said they had seen me on television and thought I might be a good candidate to try it out. It wasn't a cure for paralysis, but she explained that by wearing it under my clothes I would actually be able to stand and walk.

They offered to fly my parents and me out there immediately for a couple days to see what it was and to see if we'd be interested in participating in their long-term program. I talked to Mom and Dad and we decided it was worth checking out. What did we have to lose?

We flew out there, met with Dr. Douglas and took a look at the brace. I was surprised at how small it was. A piece of plastic wrapped around each of my calves and extended up the side of each leg to my knees. A piece of metal then ran from the knees up the side of my legs and to my chest. There were locks at my knees and hips to hold everything in place at those points. A strap then ran across my waist and chest to help hold the brace in place at those levels of my body. All of that plastic and metal may sound cumbersome, but it really wasn't. It was flexible enough to wear and fit easily underneath my clothes.

Once it was on and secure, I could stand up and, using a walker, take some steps. It wasn't easy. Considering I hadn't walked in more than a year and a half, I didn't expect it to be. But it really did work. Dr. Douglas explained that in order for me to take full advantage of it, though, I needed to use it for several consecutive months. He wanted to know if we'd commit to that. It meant I would have to move to Los Angeles for about three months, do school work out there and miss a portion of my senior year, but the decision was easy.

In May 2000 I was going to receive my high school diploma, and I decided that I was going to walk across the stage to get it. That brace was my best chance to be able to do that, so we told Dr. Douglas we'd be back in mid-August to start. I attended school on the first day of the school year, then flew the next day to Los Angeles with Mom, Dad, Mandy, and Christie where we would live until mid November. It was the chance of a lifetime, and I couldn't wait to do it.

Going out there was a win-win situation. For me, it was a chance to do something doctors told me I'd never do again. For Dynamics, it was an opportunity to show off their invention using someone who had become a fairly well-known paraplegic. If it worked for me, it could change my life for the better and mean good business for them. Because of that, they paid for the brace and all the therapy I had to go through while I was there. We had to pay for our living expenses, which we were able to do thanks to the medical fund that was established with all the money I had received from people around the world after the shooting.

Everything Dynamics had me do was gradual. They had me lift weights to build up my muscles for the entire first month. Once they felt I was strong enough, they had me put on the brace and work on standing up using parallel bars. I always had to have something to hold on to in order to keep my balance. After doing that for several days, they let me start taking steps while holding on to the bars. From that I graduated to using a walker. Then they had me try to use crutches, but I wasn't strong enough to do that. Honestly, I was happy enough with the walker, and I seemed to do that very well.

I had to use my arms and upper body a great deal to get my legs to move forward. It was tiring and I couldn't go more than a handful of steps at a time before needing a break, but I was doing it! I worked on that all day and every day, five days a week. It was the same routine each day: eat breakfast, go to Dynamics, return to the hotel in the late afternoon to do some school work, eat dinner, and go to bed.

Mandy and I were basically home schooled while we were out there. Our assignments from school were emailed to us and we did a little bit each day. The only person outside the family to help was a French tutor we hired. The original intent was for Mandy and me to teach ourselves French using CDs, but that was just too difficult for us.

When we arrived home in November, Mandy and I started school again. The students and staff had a big welcome-home party for us, and I demonstrated what I learned in Los Angeles by walking with my brace and walker in front of the whole school at an assembly in the gym. I received a standing ovation! *Good Morning America* was there to tape it, and I was happy they were. It gave me a chance to show the world just how far I'd come in two years. I used that walker as much as I could the rest of the school year, going from class to class. It was exhausting, but liberating.

After nearly two years of relying solely on a wheelchair, it was nice to have the option of walking, even if it was with a walker. The wheelchair wasn't gone from my life, but the hope was there that it might be one day. To be able to actually stand up and look someone in the face was a great feeling. I had made a lot of different investments of my time since the shooting – at Lourdes, Cardinal Hill, the summer camp in Alabama, Dynamics – and every one of those places seemed to be a piece toward my goal of one day walking again on my own.

Everything seemed to be going as well as possible for me but, as always, the ride was never completely smooth. Toward the end of my stay in California and in my first few weeks home, I faced one of the biggest and most unexpected bumps in my road to recovery: Michael started sending me letters and calling my home from jail. Eight times he would try to contact me. Six of those times were by mail and two times by phone. I never imagined it would be so easy for him to do. The letters and phone calls were intriguing, disturbing, bizarre, sad, funny. You name the emotion, and I felt it. It all happened in about a six-week period and probably would have continued if I hadn't put an end to it.

14

LETTERS FROM MICHAEL

My sister Pam and my Aunt Sissy back in Paducah gathered our mail every couple of weeks, boxed it up and sent it to us while we were in Los Angeles. A few weeks into October one of those boxes arrived. I sifted through the letters and stopped when I found a white envelope addressed to me. It was postmarked October 15, 1999, and had my name and address neatly typed. The return address had a large picture of a cross. It was from a post office box in Crittenden, Kentucky, with the name "Michael C."

"What on earth is this?" I said to nobody in particular as I opened it.

I reached inside and pulled out a couple small pieces of paper with Bible verses on them. On a regular sheet of paper was a hand-made drawing of a prison-cell door with the words "Life Behind Bars" sketched on it. There was a poem about life in prison and a page-and-a-half typed letter from Michael. A range of positive and negative thoughts bounced around in my head. My heart was racing. I knew what it was, but I still didn't believe it. I held it for a moment, took a deep breath and read it:

"Dear Melissa, Hello. How are you doing? I regret to tell you that I am doing fine. I don't know where to start. I guess I should start with an 'I'm sorry.'"

He said he was in what they called a "youth development center" and was getting help for his problems, but then contradicted that in the next couple of sentences by saying that the prison system wasn't interested in treating him, only punishing him. He said he'd found God, tried not to do anything bad there and helped people when he could. He talked about a dance he went to with a bunch of girls but was questioning whether or not he deserved to have fun.

He said he attempted suicide twice – once with a razor and once by drinking cleaning fluid – and didn't feel like he deserved to live for what he did. The doctors, he said, put him on medication to help relieve him of paranoid fears of people and monsters always watching him – fears that he claimed he'd been having before the shooting and that he said he was too embarrassed to tell anyone about. Toward the end of the letter he recalled the sentencing, saying that he was glad to see me that day and to hear what I had to say to him, but didn't appreciate much of anything else he heard.

"Do you think that some of those people were a little bit harsh," he wrote, referring to the others who spoke in court that day. *"I guess it comes with the territory."*

He concluded by asking me to send him pictures of myself.

I put the letter down and was very confused about how I felt about it. In one sense I was happy to have gotten it. I was glad to hear that he felt comfortable with me in the courtroom and that he listened to what I had to say that day. It made me feel like my words weren't wasted, and that I gave him something to think about while he serves his time. But in another sense, I felt weird and scared. How could he think what anybody said to him was harsh after what he did to them? He murdered three girls and almost murdered me and my sister. And to top it off, now he was confiding in me? I wasn't sure I wanted that. But I had more to read to help me decide that. I dug deeper into the box of mail and found two more letters from him.

The second letter was dated October 19, just four days after the first one. He included a sketch of a rose on top of a heart. The letter was typed on some unusual stationery with a border of hearts, roses, and lips. He started with a poem about friendship, love, and trust, then went right into his letter:

"...*I am sorry. I say that over and over. I hope that you believe me. The psychologist here says that I needed someone that I could write to and talk about my feelings. I hope you turn out to be that person.*"

He said that I could visit him, write to him, and that he hoped that I wasn't too mad at him for what he did to me. And that was about it. It was probably the shortest of the letters he sent.

After reading it, I still wasn't sure what exactly to do or how I should feel. Should I be flattered because he trusted me, or just completely creeped out? I was leaning more toward being creeped out. I believed him when he said he was sorry. As I've said before, I always thought before the shooting that he was a nice person, and I never believed he was aiming for me when he fired the gun. But this was way more than I needed to deal with. I was in Los Angeles learning to walk. I still had a lot of fun times to look forward to my senior year at Heath. As sincere as I thought he might be, I wasn't in the mood to be his friend. I didn't need his friendship.

The third letter was dated October 19, just like the second one. In it was a copy of a cover of a book titled "Doing Time." The letter was typed on stationery that had a dragon across the top and a smiley face at the bottom. He started, and I'm not sure why, by listing some historical events that happened on the day he wrote it. Then he wrote:

"Dear Missy, Can I call you that? I'm not sure if I'm deserving enough. When is your birthday? How are you doing? I am doing fine. I hope all is well in Paducah. Everyone here calls it P-town."

This letter seemed to be all over the board. He talked about fights in the jail that he witnessed; he said multiple times that he was sorry; again he asked for photos of me. He said he had started cursing more and more because the other convicts were rubbing off on him; he was willing to let me run him over with a car, shoot him and torture him if he got out of prison; he was being tested for AIDS; and he met girls in jail with sexually transmitted diseases.

That letter was all I needed to be certain that I should not write back to him. I pretty much knew after reading the second letter that I wasn't going to respond to him, but this third one confirmed it. Each letter I read seemed stranger and stranger. Yes, he apologized some more, but I didn't need to know about the fights or the girls or the AIDS testing. What was that all about?

I also worried that if I wrote back and he suddenly got better through our correspondence that someone on his side might say "Look! He's contacted one of his victims and they're getting along, so he's cured! He should be freed!" I know now how crazy that was to think that way but, as a 17 year old, I had no idea what writing to him might lead to. Soon after reading those first three letters, our stay in California was over and we went back home. I wanted to put the letters all behind me and get back to my friends and life in Paducah. I had hoped that was the last I would hear from him, but it wasn't.

When we got home, Michael continued to disrupt my life – first with a phone call, then with another letter. The phone call was a message left on our answering machine while we were in California. He told me who he was and that he wanted to see how I was doing.

Hearing his voice made me very uncomfortable, and I
was glad I wasn't home when he called. The letter there
waiting for me was postmarked November 5. He wrote
"Apology Enclosed" on the outside of the envelope,
included a full-page picture of Albert Einstein and typed
the letter on stationery that had some hearts and dol-
phins on it. He began with:

"Missy, Hey girl. What's going down? Not much here.
Just thinking about you. But that's nothing new."

He said he didn't blame me if I never wanted to
contact him, and that he was writing to me so that I
would understand him better and because his psychologist said it would help him. He said he loved me as
a friend and, once again, apologized. He claimed that he
had been saved by God and that he hoped I found
comfort in God.

"I am sick. I need help. I think you can give me the help
that I need. I hope that you understand what I am saying."

He then shifted gears and said he was trying to call
his sister one night, but ended up dialing the wrong
number and talking to a girl named Abby who was
folding clothes. He then asked what kind of music I
liked, asked me how old I was and asked for my views
on reformatories before ending with another "I'm sorry."

OK, so the first letter started with "Dear, Melissa,
Hello. How are you doing?" and now it was "Hey girl.
What's going down?" It's like he thought we were best
friends or something. Was he trying different approaches
to try to get me to respond, or was his writing just based
on whatever mood he was in at the time? Despite some
of the rambling he did and how chummy he was trying
to be, I was still going through that wide range of
emotions.

In this letter he said "Just thinking about you. But
that's nothing new." Part of me found that disturbing,
but another part of me still felt sad for him. This letter to
me seemed like a cry for help more than the previous

letters. He even mentioned that he thought I could be the one to give him the help that he needed. But I still didn't give in. I felt like he was giving me a huge responsibility that I shouldn't have had to bear. I had my own issues to deal with at the time. I couldn't take on his.

The fifth letter was sent November 15. It included poems about limbo and about being a prisoner. There was also a clipping he got from a publication written by an Ohio prisoner about how long prison times only make inmates worse. The letter was typed on stationery that had pictures of different breeds of dogs on it.

He told me that he'd read an article about me on the Internet that I was visiting a doctor in California, and he hoped that it was going well. He then reflected on the sentencing and what Kelly had said to him in the court-room that day – that she didn't care if he was sorry and that she felt he deserved to die.

"I kind of agree with her. You know **I DESERVE TO DIE.** *But,* **IT DOES MATTER IF I AM SORRY!** *I hope you understand what I am saying. I do care about you."*

He followed that with his strongest effort yet to get me to contact him by saying that his counselor told him I wanted to contact him, and that I could visit him if I could get a ride to the jail. He also enclosed a stamp so that I could write him back.

He talked about pursing an education from jail, and that he thought he was "stupid" until he got there and found out that many of his prison mates couldn't read or write. He said that made him realize that he shouldn't take things for granted, such as the freedom to eat, shower, and choose your hair style.

"I guess when you take others' freedoms away from them, then the government takes yours away. Seems fair doesn't it?"

He closed by asking me, again, to send him photos of me.

He tugged at my emotions a bit with this letter because he brought up some issues that I actually agreed with. While Kelly and I were and still are best friends, I didn't agree with what she said at the sentencing that he should die for what he did. Why not make him stay in prison forever and make him think every day about what he did to us? I'm sure in many ways a prison is hell in itself. I was also intrigued by what he said about not taking things for granted. I've said that exact same thing a million times. It's sad in his case that he didn't think of that before he killed or injured eight people, but hopefully it's a lesson that other people thinking about committing a crime like his will consider.

And for the record, I never sent him any photos like he requested several times, and I never told anybody that I wanted to go up and visit him. I don't know if somebody really told him that or if he was just hoping. I couldn't even get myself to write back to him at that time, let alone see him.

Soon after getting that fifth letter he called our house again. I wasn't home but my dad answered the phone. Michael asked for me and Dad, not knowing initially to whom he was talking, told him I was out. Michael then started saying, "I'm sorry! I'm sorry!" as many times as he could before Dad realized it was him and calmly hung up the phone.

Within days after that another letter postmarked November 29 was received, right around the two-year anniversary of the shooting. That's when I decided enough was enough. Mom and Dad and the rest of the family had pretty much stayed out of giving their opinions on the letters. They let me make my own decisions on what to do with them but always let me know they were there if I needed some advice. Well, I called on my parents to help after I got this one. The outside of the envelope had the words "I'm sorry" scribbled all over it. I felt what was inside the envelope was going to be much of the same as the others, so I decided to not even open it. I was done with him. Six letters and two phone calls in about six weeks was too much. I'd made up my mind a while ago that I wasn't going to respond, so why let him play with my emotions by allowing him to write to me or call me every week or more?

The next morning my parents and I went to Tim Kaltenbach, the attorney who prosecuted the case, and gave him all the letters. We asked him to contact Michael's attorney and the prison to put a stop to the letters and the phone calls, and he did.

What was interesting about the sixth and last letter was that I didn't read it until I started this book, about nine years after Michael wrote it. It included a picture of roses, a picture of himself, a caricature of a gorilla eating a banana with the caption "BIG DADDY?" and a poem about God. It was a very bizarre combination of items, and also was the first letter he sent me that was hand-written. It was fairly short and focused on God more than any other letter he'd sent.

"If you ever get down, just remember Jeremiah 29:11. You have a future and a hope," he wrote.

He said he wasn't an atheist before the shooting, something that had been reported by some in the media. He said he just felt so low and helpless that he didn't think even God could help him, but now realized he was wrong.

"I sinned and god is the only one who forgives me," he said. *"He gives you and your family the strength to forgive me."*

He quoted a scripture he said he got out of a Bible that says he who hates his brother is a murderer, and no murderer has eternal life.

"So don't hate me," he said. *"You can dislike me if you want."*

Looking back on the letters and phone calls, I don't really blame him for trying to contact me. It wasn't the smartest decision in the world, but he probably figured that it was 10 months after the sentencing (which I'm sure seemed a lot longer to him than it did to me). Since I wasn't mean to him at the sentencing, and we got along well before the shooting, why not give it a shot? But it was too much for me at the time.

Could I have helped him if I had written back? Maybe, but I don't see how it could have helped me. I don't mean to sound selfish, but I had enough to worry about with my condition. The last thing I needed was to be a counselor at the age of 17 to the person who put me in the position I was in. He needed help, but he needed to go elsewhere to get it. Maybe several years down the road I would be open to talking to him, and maybe even meeting with him, but not at that time.

With the letters and phone calls stopped, I was able to concentrate on myself again. I had a lot to look forward to my senior year, and a tremendous amount of work to do. Specifically, I needed to pick a college.

I discovered something about myself while in Los Angeles: I was really a city girl who had been born and raised in the country. I loved L.A. I felt like I fit in with the bright lights and fast pace of everything. In fact, I loved it so much that I took a tour of the University of Southern California campus when I was out there and decided that was where I was going to attend college. Mandy felt the same way and decided USC was for her, too. That didn't make my mom too happy since it was 2,000 miles away from home. She'd do her best to try to talk us out of it in the coming months. I was going to have a difficult decision to make as my high school years – probably some of the strangest high school years any teenager ever had to go through – came to a conclusion.

15

FAREWELL TO HEATH

The main reason Mom didn't want Mandy and me to go to college in California was because she said she couldn't handle having three of her daughters out there, so far away from her. Three daughters? Yes, because that would soon be Christie's new home.

During our stay in Los Angeles, Christie, Mandy, and I spent some evenings on the Internet in various chat rooms talking to some local people. One night Christie started chatting with a guy named Dave and asked him questions such as where we could go for fun. The next thing we knew, Dave was asking her to meet him somewhere. Unsure of who this guy was, but curious and interested at the same time, Christie decided to meet him in a populated place such as a mall and only if Mandy and I would go with her. We did – and it was the last time Christie wanted us to go along. She and Dave hit it off immediately and started dating. In no time they were in love with each other.

When we returned to Paducah in November, Christie and Dave continued to stay in touch. About eight months later, Christie moved to California and they became engaged. They were married soon after and lived in

California for about five years. Today they are living in
Tennessee, happily married now for about nine years.

The relationship between Christie and Dave is a
perfect example of my belief that everything happens
for a reason. Had I not been shot and paralyzed, I never
would have had any reason to go to Los Angeles. Had I
not had a reason to go California, Christie would not
have gone there. She and Dave would have never met.
Was I meant to get shot so that Christie and Dave could
live happily ever after? I doubt that was God's sole or
primary reason, but there's no reason to believe that it
wasn't one of His purposes.

So back to Mandy and me and USC – do we go there
or look for a school closer to home? Mom practically
begged us to look at Murray State University in Murray,
Kentucky. It was a really nice school of about 9,000
students in a quaint college town of only about 15,000
people, but it was just 45 minutes southeast of Paducah.[48]
That was a little closer to home than I wanted. After
going through all I had with the shooting, I was looking
forward to a fresh start a little farther away, somewhere
outside of Kentucky. But that didn't happen.

Mom told us to at least visit Murray and give it a
chance. She said we could always go to graduate school
in California if we still had a desire in four years to go
out there. Our school counselor also mentioned Murray
State and told us not to limit our college visits to just
USC. And then there was my friend, Kelly, who decided
she was going to Murray State and did all she could to
talk us into going there with her.

So to appease everybody, Mandy and I reluctantly
decided to visit the school in early 2000. Much to our
surprise, we liked it a lot. I didn't know yet what I
wanted to major in, but because of the shooting I knew
I wanted to do something that would involve helping
children. Social work and psychology were two possibilities, and Murray State had good programs in those

areas. It was also a very pretty campus, and I started to think that being so close to home might not be such a bad thing after all. I still loved USC and the thought of living in sunny Southern California, but the bond with my family and friends was just too strong. Murray State it was going to be!

Despite all of the college talk, I still had the second half of my senior year to enjoy. In February I attended a Valentine's Day dance at our school with a sophomore I didn't even know. He had been home schooled since about fifth grade but attended Heath that year and was extremely shy. Instead of walking up to me and asking me if I would go to the dance with him, he had someone pass me a note in class that asked if I would go with him. The note had instructions that said to answer him by circling either "yes" or "no." Was this for real? Not only was that a bit odd at our age, but I had to ask someone to point him out to me because I had no clue who he was. I didn't hold any of that against him, though. I wasn't dating anyone at the time and figured what the heck, going with him might be fun.

So I picked him up – yes, I drove because he didn't have his license, and we went to the dance. When it was over, he asked me if we could drive around for a while. So we did. Then he asked if we could go park somewhere just to talk. So we did, at a nearby park that had a real pretty pond. Then he asked me if I would teach him how to kiss. Uh, what? I had no idea how to answer that question. But he was a really sweet guy who seemed harmless, and he did muster up the courage to ask, so I taught him. But that was as far as it went. I took him home after his kissing lesson and that was the end of it.

As one might expect, given the lack of dating experience he had and the kissing we did, he ended up having a pretty big crush on me after that, but there were no more dates. It was a fun and interesting evening, but I didn't feel anything more for him other than a friendship. Hopefully the night gave him some social confidence. That's all he really needed. He was certainly a nice enough guy.

A few weeks later I packed up and headed back to Los Angeles again with my family for about a month. One reason was to spend some more time working with the brace. The main reason, though, was to show off that brace by participating in the Los Angeles Marathon. I was one of about ten people in it wearing a Dynamics brace. The race was such a huge event for the city with thousands of participants running the 26.2-mile course. Of course, my trek was going to be far shorter – about a quarter of a mile with the aid of the brace and a walker. It doesn't sound long, but it was farther than I had walked at any time since the shooting, and I earned every step of it.

It was a cold, rainy day and I had to take several breaks along the way. The walk was extremely grueling. There were times when I knew I'd make it to the finish line. And then there were times when I was ready to call it quits. I was happy, fatigued, upset, and excited. I ran the gamut when it came to emotions that morning. But in the end, I made it. When I crossed the finish line, I was swarmed by reporters. One would have thought I just completed and won the entire marathon by the way they were acting. But I appreciated the attention. I answered their questions, smiled for the cameras, then did what I had done a lot of the past two-plus years: I sat down in my wheelchair. I was exhausted!

We returned home from Los Angeles in April. I went to school to wrap up my class work for the year and had three big events in May to look forward to: the Million Mom March, senior prom, and graduation.

The Million Mom March that year was the first ever, held May 14 in Washington, D.C. The purpose of that grassroots movement was to raise awareness of the lack of rational gun laws in our country. I saw so many famous people that day: Rosie O'Donnell, Susan Sarandon, and Melissa Etheridge, to name a few. I wasn't there to just march but to actually speak. My turn was brief. I just read a quick fact about guns from a card I had been given, but what an experience! I went up to the podium set up on the National Mall and looked out in awe. The crowd was estimated at 750,000![49] And all eyes, at least those close enough, were on me. It was nerve-wracking, but I read my card without a hitch.

While some people in the Million Mom March each year may be against any civilian having a gun, I don't share that belief. I'm not against people owning guns. I never was before the shooting and haven't been since. But I do believe guns and ammunition should be locked up securely enough that children have no way of getting to them. For someone to own guns and not take the proper precautions and responsibility for them is where I believe many of today's problems with guns lie. Look how easy it was for Michael and the shooters at Pearl, Jonesboro, and Columbine to get guns. It should never be that easy for a teenager or child.

I returned home from the march in time for my senior prom, which turned out to be as wonderful as a senior prom could be. I attended with a guy named Matt from another school whom I'd dated briefly before and after the prom. The anticipated night got off to a great start several weeks earlier when Mandy and I received a phone call from Hollywood fashion designers Nolan Miller and Mark Zunino, who were well known for making dresses for film and television stars. They had seen us on television and wanted to make us dresses for the prom at no charge. How could we turn that down?

I picked one out that was similar to that worn to the Oscars by Nancy O'Dell, one of the hosts of the show "Access Hollywood." The dress was red and black and required the satin material to be shipped in from another country. The designers spared no expense! I have no

idea how much it cost, but I'm sure if we would have had to pay for them the price would have been thousands of dollars. We were so appreciative of their generosity – and looked pretty darn good, too!

The dance itself was a lot of fun. It was pretty much a typical dance, which is what I enjoyed about it. *Good Morning America* was there to tape it but, unlike the year before with the photographer following us around all night, I wouldn't allow them in the dance. I told them they could tape us at dinner and outside the dance, which I cleared with my date first, but that was where I was drawing the line. The *Good Morning America* crew was very amicable about it. In fact, they were so appreciative I let them tape as much as I did that they paid for our limousine and dinner. I gave them an interview the next day and talked about the dance itself, and everyone was happy. It was a very relaxing, memorable evening as my days at Heath wound down

Finally, there was graduation. It was a ceremony that was memorable in so many ways. Every graduation ceremony is a big deal to the students, parents, and school staff involved just because of what it is: four years of hard work coming to an end, and the beginning of the next phases of our lives. But the graduation for the Heath class of 2000 had much more drama than a typical ceremony, with two very unforgettable moments.

One of those moments was when the school gave Kayce Steger's diploma to her parents. A seat was left open among us: the one Kayce would have occupied if she were alive – with a red rose placed on it. Kayce was the only one from our class killed that day, and we weren't going to let her be forgotten on the most important day of our high school years. She should have been there with us, but since she wasn't, we were going to keep her memory alive. It was terribly sad to see that empty chair and to watch her parents go up there instead of her. There wasn't a dry eye in the place. It brought back so many memories – good memories about her, and bad memories about what happened to her. But it was the right tribute on the part of the school and district administrators to honor her as they did.

The other memorable moment was when I fulfilled my goal of walking up to receive my diploma. The stage was so high that I needed some help getting on it – OK, a lot of help – in the form of a forklift raising me in my wheelchair onto the stage! It was pretty embarrassing, but certainly broke any tension and nervousness I may have had. Once I was lowered onto the stage with my brace on underneath my gown, Mandy and Christie were there to help me stand up. Once I got up, I used my walker to walk across the stage to receive my diploma.

To try to describe the elation I felt is impossible. It was a huge accomplishment and one of the most memorable times in my life since I became a paraplegic. I received a standing ovation that seemed to go on forever. When I walked to the end of the stage, I sat down in my chair and the forklift lowered me to the floor. Waiting for me with a bouquet of flowers were the doctors from Dynamics. *Good Morning America* and the *Today Show* were there to capture it all. It was a good way to end an otherwise tumultuous high school career.

When I looked back at my high school years, I realized that I really didn't have much of a high school life, at least not like most kids have. I was there my entire freshman year and junior year, but that was it. I missed more than half of my sophomore year and a significant portion of my senior year. I felt cheated out of what were supposed to be some of the most memorable years of my life – memorable in a positive way, I mean

– but there was really no point in fretting over it. What happened had happened.

The situation was what God wanted, and I think I made the best of it. Not only that, but I knew some of the best years of my life were just around the corner awaiting me at Murray State. I was going to be on my own more than ever before, and I was looking forward to it. Anything that was taken away from me in high school because of the shooting: my freedom, my education, time with my friends – would be made up for in college. I was ready to keep living.

— A much anticipated day —

Mandy behind me and Kelly Hard standing behind Mandy

16

AL GORE AND COLLEGE
COME CALLING

The summer of 2000, my last summer break before starting college, was expected to be uneventful from start to finish. I didn't work. I had no interviews or television appearances to make. I had an orientation day at Murray State to attend, but that was about it. I planned to just hang out with my friends and have some fun, and that's pretty much the way it went in June and July – until I received a phone call one day at the end of July from a staff member on Vice President Al Gore's presidential campaign.

With President Clinton about to leave office after two terms, Vice President Gore was running against George W. Bush in the upcoming November election. The Democratic National Convention was being held in August at the Staples Center in Los Angeles. Mr. Gore wanted me to be a part of it by speaking about my experiences since the shooting to the convention crowd and the live, prime-time television audience across the country. The convention was taking place just days before college started, but how could I say no to such an invitation?

I was 18 years old at the time and not much into politics. I came from a family full of Democrats, so I considered myself a Democrat. But I'd never voted, never campaigned for anybody, and really hadn't paid much attention to politicians or their views on various issues.

Some people in Paducah who knew me from church asked me not to go to the convention when they found out about my invitation because of Mr. Gore's stances on certain issues that may have conflicted with my faith, but whether or not I agreed with him on every issue was not important to me. What I knew for sure was that he knew who I was, knew what happened to me, and he knew how I'd come back from that tragic day. He wanted me to share that story with the country, and I was happy to do so. Simply put, I accepted Mr. Gore's invitation because he asked. Had Mr. Bush asked me to speak at the Republican convention, I'd have been there, too.

I flew to Los Angeles with my parents and Mandy the day before I was scheduled to speak. I had such a fun time mingling with various celebrities and dignitaries. I didn't get to meet Mr. Gore because he was not yet at the convention, but there were several famous people – at least to me – whom I got to meet. One was pro wrestler Dwayne Johnson, also known as "The Rock." Another was Pat Morita, who played Mr. Miyagi in the *Karate Kid* movies. I grew up watching those movies and recognized him as soon as I saw him. He and I had something in common at the convention: we were both in wheelchairs. He was only in his late 60s at the time but had been in pretty poor health. He died of natural causes five years later at the age of 73.[50]

I was scheduled to speak on Tuesday evening, August 15. Everything was set. I was going to talk about the day of the shooting, how I'd refused to let it keep me down, and how important it was for kids to speak up when they heard of any threat of violence in school. But as oftentimes happens in huge, live events like the convention, plans changed at the last minute. Due to time constraints, I was told I would get to go on stage, but not to speak. Instead, they showed a video of some of my rehabilitation back home and a short speech I'd taped earlier in the day. That was shown to the crowd and on national television, followed by me walking on stage using my brace. I received a long, standing ovation. It was such an exhilarating feeling to be out there on my feet in front of all those people and in front of the millions of people watching on television. I was disappointed that I couldn't speak live to everybody, but I couldn't complain about the opportunity they gave me.

About three years earlier, all anybody knew about me was that I would likely never walk again. But at the convention, they saw me walk. If what I did that night inspired just one person to believe in himself or herself and accomplish something he or she never thought possible, or if it encouraged one person to speak up about potential violence, or if it pushed someone who was having personal problems to get some help rather than taking his or her anger out on others, then it was well worth it.

We flew home from Los Angeles and were excited to pack and head to Murray. College was going to be one of the biggest changes of my life for many reasons, but none bigger than the fact that, for the first time, I was not going to be living with Mandy. She and I decided that college would be a great opportunity to see how well we could do without each other. No, we weren't completely going our separate ways. Far from it. Mandy was going to live with a girl named Kelli Watson with whom we attended high school, and I was going to live with Kelly Hard, but our rooms were right across the hall from each other on the first floor of one of the dormitories. It may not sound like a big deal to many, but after living with each other and doing everything together for all 18-plus years of our lives, living apart for the first time was a monumental step.

I also pushed the envelope a little further when I decided to rush a sorority while Mandy and Kelly decided not to. At first they were going to rush, but for some reason changed their minds. I pushed them to rush with me, but they didn't budge. I boldly decided, though, that wasn't going to stop me from doing it. College was where I was going to meet a lot of new people and make some friends for life, so why not start meeting new people right out of the gate? It was something I knew would make me stronger and more independent. It was a great opportunity that I didn't want to pass up.

I rushed all five sororities on campus and didn't get dropped by any of them. That meant it was basically my choice of which one I wanted to join. Sororities were big on promoting how diverse they were, and I was the only one in a wheelchair rushing that year, but I don't think that played a factor in all of them wanting me. They may have been thinking that way when they first saw me and didn't know me, but once they learned more about me as a person, hopefully they all legitimately liked me for who I was rather than what I was.

I eventually decided on Alpha Omicron Pi because I already knew a few people in that sorority from high school and felt the most comfortable with them. When the initiation was over, Mandy and Kelly said they wished they had rushed with me. Of course, so did I! But that was fine that they didn't. There were no sorority houses, so it wasn't like we were going to be living apart. Nothing had changed between us. The only thing that changed was I had a jump on making some new friends. It was a good situation for me. Some new friends came into my life, and I still had my old ones. I also proved to myself that I could do something on my own without Mandy at my side every step of the way.

Mandy and I immediately declared our majors: social work. I was lucky to even have a future, so there was no sense in wasting time deciding what I wanted to do with it. Some people have asked if I picked that career because of the shooting. The answer is a resounding "Absolutely!" I wanted to work in schools and help kids who had troubles like Michael. For whatever reason, he felt like he didn't have anybody to turn to. If he had felt like there was someone he could have confided in, what he did that day could have possibly been prevented.

My career choice was another example of good that came from the shooting. I have no idea what I would have done with my life if the shooting hadn't happened. But because it did, it gave me direction: a solid direction that had the potential to change, and maybe even save lives.

Since we declared the same majors, Mandy and I shared the same classes. The campus was pretty much accessible for handicapped people, but there was one building that sat on a steep hill. Unfortunately, it's where several of my social work classes were. Mandy always helped me get up and down, but if she didn't go to class because she was sick, I didn't go to class. That was one frustrating thing about being in a wheelchair.

I could have gone to class and probably anybody passing by or in my class would have been more than happy to help me up or down, but it was one of those things where I felt I would be bothering other people. Nobody ever made me feel that way. It's just something I had to battle in my own mind. What if I traveled across campus to the building and nobody was there to help me? What if someone did offer, but I was making that person late for his or her class? What if they hurt themselves pushing me up the hill? Maybe I had become so independent in the last few years that expecting someone besides Mandy to help me with something like that just made me too uncomfortable. It's probably something anybody in a wheelchair will tell you he or she has had to deal with at some point.

People around campus were always so nice to me, and there were a few things that I was more than happy to let them do for me that didn't require a long push up a steep hill. I never had to open a door to a building in my four-and-a-half years there. If my class had one of those desks with a chair attached to it, someone would turn the desk around for me so I could roll my wheel-chair up to it. Even people in the parking lot who saw me try to slide myself into my car offered to help. I still tried to do as much on my own as I could, but it was nice to know I had so many people around me who cared, even people who didn't know me.

Even though it was only about 45 minutes from Paducah, many students on campus were from other parts of the state or country and had no idea who I was. Some people would point and whisper when they saw me, which told me that they recognized who I was, but most didn't know me. Many people knew about the shooting and knew there was a girl who was paralyzed, but they didn't know I was that girl. As much as I liked to talk about what happened to me and didn't mind the attention I'd received for it, it was refreshing to be relatively unknown for a change. I felt like just another student on campus.

It didn't take long for me to forget about how close I came to going to USC. Murray had everything I wanted and needed: the right classes, a good group of friends and, yes, it was even nice to be close to home. Unless there was a fraternity party or something exciting happening on the weekends at Murray, I went home to Paducah a lot. While living in sunny southern California would have been a great experience, the 2,000 miles between there and home might have been a little too much. Though I was very independent in college, it was always comforting knowing that Mom and Dad were nearby if I needed them.

Though I was treated like any other student at Murray, my mini-celebrity status had not gone away off campus. In the fall of my freshman year, Mandy and I traveled to Los Angeles for a few days to appear in an episode of MTV's *Flipped*. The show, described by MTV as "a cross between *Fantasy Island* and *Scared Straight*,"[51] would turn the tables on someone. For example, the episode Mandy and I were in was about bullying.

The show took two kids who were bullies in real life and sent them to another school for a day where they were bullied mercilessly by actors, though they didn't know those bullies were actors. Mandy got to act in it as one of the few students who was actually nice to the kids who had been "flipped." My role was after the show, sharing my story with viewers. It was really a great experience and fun to be on MTV, a station I grew up watching in the 1980s and 1990s. And I'm happy to say the bullying episode is still used today around the country as a tool for counseling.

Soon after the MTV gig, I did a couple commercials for Channel One, an educational channel that is broadcast in schools nationwide. The commercials' focus was to encourage kids to speak up anytime they heard their schoolmates talking about doing something devastating like Michael did so that such a tragedy could be prevented from ever happening again.

In the winter of that year I received a few prestigious local and national honors. I was named Paducah Patriot of the Year by my city and Kentuckian of the Year by *Kentucky Monthly* magazine, both awards that I was very honored to receive. I also received an award from U.S. Attorney General Janet Reno for "work in protecting children and combating juvenile crime." I was one of fifteen people nationwide to receive that award from the Justice Department's Office of Juvenile Justice and Delinquency Prevention. I was flown to Washington, D.C., to meet Ms. Reno and be honored. According to the press release they sent out, I was "a leader in encouraging youth involvement in crime prevention."[52] I think that was based on a couple of organizations in which I was active since the shooting.

One was Youth Crime Watch of America (YCWA), where I basically told my story to children across the country through interviews. The organization started in Florida in 1979 and is now worldwide. It encourages youth to make a difference by being active in preventing crime and drugs from entering their schools and neighborhoods.

The other was PAX, a nonpolitical group that works to end gun violence. It was co-founded by Daniel Gross, whose brother, Matthew, was shot and seriously wounded by a gunman atop the Empire State Building in New York City, just a little more than nine months before I was shot. I participated (and still do) in the organization's "Speak Up" campaign, which promotes an anonymous national hot line that kids can call if they suspect there is a threat of school violence. There are several other aspects to it, including a school-based curriculum and an annual gala each spring, attended by dozens of dignitaries, where I sometimes tell my story.

Outside of YCWA and PAX, I also told my story to several middle and high school students in the region. I began speaking at those assemblies my junior year of high school, continued through college and still speak regularly today. One of my talks usually lasts about 45 minutes. I start out by telling my audience that I was a 15-year-old, typical teenager who just finished praying in a prayer circle when a 14-year-old boy pulled out a .22. At that point I can hear a pin drop in the room. Many jaws drop. I have their attention.

I then tell them what I remember from that day, what I knew about Michael, and how our lives were affected by his actions. I try to make them realize the importance of life and of not taking anything for granted. I then leave it open for questions, of which there are normally many. There is no way to know if the talks always have an effect on kids. My guess is that I get through to some of them, based on the comments I receive. But one thing I know for sure is that the talks have an effect on me. Talking about the shooting as much as I do is continuous therapy for me. Some might think it gets old, but it never does. Each time features a new audience, new questions, and the potential to reach kids who need to be reached.

Those talks were a big reason why, in the spring of 2003, I had the confidence to enter the Miss Wheelchair Kentucky Pageant. There was a student at Murray State who won the 2002 pageant and encouraged me to run. I'd never heard of it but, after some research, I decided to give it a go. The contest had been in existence since 1998. Contestants were judged on their accomplishments, communication skills, ability to deal with media, and self-perception (such as poise and demeanor).[53] I felt I handled all of those categories well, and so did the judges. There were five contestants, and I won! That sent me on to the Miss Wheelchair America Program in Iowa where there were somewhere between 25 and 30 contestants.

The evening of the national pageant, I was getting ready upstairs in my hotel room and, being the procrastinator I am, I was rushing around. All contestants had to be downstairs early where there were makeup artists waiting for us. In my mad rush, I wheeled through the bedroom and over a pair of my tennis shoes – except my wheels didn't exactly make it over the shoes. Instead, the front of the wheels elevated and the chair tipped backward. I banged my head on a wall, causing my nose to bleed, and my knees flew up and hit me square in the eyes! Can you believe that? Minutes before I was supposed to be down there getting ready to go on stage for a national competition, there I was lying on the floor with a knot on my head, a bloody nose, and two black eyes. I wish I could say it was a factor in me not winning the pageant, but I can't. The makeup ladies were able to do some pretty incredible work. Nobody even noticed I'd bruised and bloodied myself just minutes earlier. I don't know how close I came to winning (I do know I wasn't in the top three), but it was an incredible experience. To meet all of those women in wheelchairs and to be able to share our stories with each other about our disabilities was invaluable.

I got through school with decent grades of As, Bs, and an occasional C. I finished with a grade point average a little above 3.0. My internship was at a local elementary school family resource center in the fall of 2004, my final semester before graduation. We conducted various programs for at-risk children, such as fire safety, and also helped families with various everyday issues they faced, such as paying their electric bills. It was a great opportunity for me to be able to work directly with children in a real-world setting, and it got me ready for graduation.

I graduated on December 18, 2004. I didn't walk across the stage as I did in high school because I didn't want to be the center of attention. But I ended up being just that anyway. I was the first to go across the stage and received a standing ovation. And, as they were many times during my high school years, the *Good Morning America* crew was there to capture it all. Graduating meant so much to me. Mandy and I were the first of my parents' six children to earn college degrees.

And then, of course, there was the shooting factor. On December 18, 1997, I was in Lourdes Hospital with absolutely no clue of what my future held. I didn't know if I'd even finish high school, let alone go to college. But seven years later, there I was on stage receiving my diploma.

If it seems like I breezed through talking about my college years, it's because those years weren't a whole lot different or any more exciting than anybody else's college experience. Mandy and I did perfectly fine not living together. I went to my classes, participated in various activities with my sorority sisters, and went to campus parties or back home on the weekends. Outside of the awards I received in 2000 and my appearance on MTV, I was just another college student at Murray. This I was very happy about.

But I did leave out one very important and interesting topic: the college dating scene. While I tried to distance myself from boys in high school after the shooting because of all the personal issues I had to deal with that I didn't want to tell them about, I was the complete opposite in college. I dated a lot and told many of my boyfriends all about those embarrassing things that came with being a paraplegic. I also was fortunate enough, in my junior year, to meet a guy who would be the last person I would ever date. I knew almost immediately after I met him that Josh Smith was "the one."

17

MY GUY

I talked earlier about how I didn't date much in high school after the shooting because of the complications I faced, such as going to the bathroom, that I wasn't comfortable revealing to boys. I also wasn't convinced they were dating me for reasons other than the fact that I was that girl who was shot at Heath High School. But my attitude changed when I got to Murray State.

I had a few different boyfriends my first two-plus years there and I didn't hesitate, after getting to know them a bit, to tell them what I had to deal with: the cathing, wetting myself on occasion, and sometimes having to wear diapers.

Why did I start to date again in college and open up about all of that? One reason was that many students at Murray State were from various places outside of the region. They didn't know me as the girl who got shot in nearby Paducah. They knew me simply as a college girl named Missy Jenkins. They dated me for who I was, not what I was. That made it so much easier to go out with them and to trust their intentions. And I never felt like the wheelchair was something that came between us. In fact, most of them even made the comment that, after a while, they didn't even notice the wheelchair. They might have asked questions about my condition, which was fine, but it was never an issue that came between us.

Another reason I opened up was maturity. Yes, I know college students can be immature when they want to be, but there's something between that last year of high school and first year of college that usually makes people grow up a little bit. Maybe it's being away from home and having a larger burden of responsibility with which to deal in order to survive. Maybe it's simply being a year older and, thus, the realization that they're a year closer to entering the real world. Whatever the reason, the guys I dated in college were much more mature, as was I, and I knew they could handle what I had to tell them.

While I enjoyed those relationships I had my first couple of years at Murray, none of them worked out. A couple lasted a few months each. One lasted more than a year. But there were compatibility problems in all of them. We tried to make them work, but they just weren't meant to be. When each of those breakups occurred, I wondered when I would finally find "the one."

Fortunately, I didn't have to wait too long to get my answer. It was my junior year – February 24, 2003 – when I was at a fraternity party that I didn't want to attend at a ridiculous hour of the night, all because a friend from out of town wanted to go. But had I not gone, I may have never met Josh.

The out-of-town friend was a girl named Nora, who attended Western Kentucky University. She came to visit Mandy and me for a weekend and didn't arrive until about three o'clock that Saturday morning, but she insisted that we go find a party somewhere on campus as soon as she got there. I was very tired and didn't want to go anywhere but, since she was my guest and because that's what she wanted to do, I obliged.

We went to the Pi Kappa Alpha fraternity house where there was a party going on. We bumped into some friends of ours and were out on the dance floor talking. We were having a good time when, suddenly, I noticed a guy sitting on a stool across the room staring at me. It was obvious what he was doing: giving me that "I think you're cute" kind of look. So I played along and returned it with my own "I think you're cute" kind of look. Having established with our eyes that we were attracted to each other, he walked up to a friend, asked him who I was and told him that he wanted to talk to me. But his friend told him not to. Why not? He wouldn't say, he just insisted that he not talk to me. So the guy went back to the stool, sat down, and continued to stare at me. Finally, after a few minutes and ignoring his friend's advice, he came over and talked to me.

"Hi, I'm Josh Smith," he said.

"Hi, I'm Missy Jenkins," I replied with a smile.

So we were attracted to each other and knew who the other was. What was next? Well, his first question to me was, "Why did my friend tell me not to come over and talk to you?" It turned out that friend had another friend who liked me, and he didn't want Josh to upset that guy. What mattered, though, at least from my perspective, was that I was not attracted to that other friend. I knew he liked me, but there was and never had been any special feelings there. I liked him as a friend, but that was it. I was glad Josh came over and introduced himself.

Unfortunately, our conversation didn't last long. Josh's friends were leaving, and he had already told them he'd go out with them. He didn't know where they were going, but he wanted to talk with me some more. We exchanged phone numbers.

"Call me when you get back to your place," he said.

"But it's already late, and I don't know when I'll be back there," I replied.

"I don't care what time it is," he said. "I want you to call me."

Mandy, Nora, and I left the fraternity house and went to someone else's house where there was a party. We hung out there for about an hour-and-a-half before heading home. It was 6 A.M. when we got back. I was so tired and was ready to crash when I remembered Josh had told me to call him. I pulled out his number and wondered if I should. He told me he had his own room at the frat house, so I knew I wouldn't be waking others up if I called his phone. So I called him.

I dialed...it rang...and then Josh answered. Except he was sound asleep. Honestly, I don't even know how he was conscious enough to pick up the phone because when he picked it up, he was snoring into it. No words. Not even an incoherent mumble. Just loud, heavy breathing. I tried to wake him up, but to no avail. I hung up and decided if he wanted to talk to me, he could call me later that day. Not exactly a great start to a potential relationship, but it was 6 A.M., and we'd both been up all night. I gave him the benefit of the doubt.

All day Sunday went by without a phone call, but he finally called me that night when I was studying at the library. He asked if we could get together Monday, and I agreed. He arrived and had brought the movie *The Outsiders*. I was ready for a relaxing, enjoyable evening and a chance to get to know him. But instead, I ended up wondering if the relationship was meant to be. That's because just minutes after he got there our doorbell rang, and it was the other fellow who liked me: the one I liked just as a friend. I had no idea he was coming over, and his timing couldn't have been worse. He came inside and made himself at home.

Thank goodness Kelly was there. She talked to Josh and carried on a nice conversation with him while I tried to politely get this other friend to leave. He finally left after what seemed like an eternity and Josh, noticeably

irritated, asked if he should go, too. I told him no. I
wanted him to stay, and I was sorry for the unexpected
interruption. So we finally started the movie but hadn't
gotten very far into it when Josh suddenly fell asleep!
Right there on my couch! He felt bad when I finally
woke him up to go home. I felt terrible about the slow
start to the evening. So we agreed to try again Tuesday
night, and I'm glad we did because, finally, everything
clicked.

It was just a simple evening of talking and getting to
know each other better, but there was no doubt in either
of our minds that there was some serious chemistry
there. We felt like we had known each other our entire
lives. We were so interested in each other. I told him
about my life, and he told me about his. We asked each
other a lot of questions. He was a lifelong Murray
resident, played football in high school, and grew up on
a tobacco farm. He wanted to be a physical education
teacher. From my perspective he had it all: looks, brains,
and even a planned future.

Our start was rocky those first couple of days, but it
improved every single day after that. We immensely
enjoyed each other's company and wanted to be together all the time. This was the man of my dreams, and
I knew it. I was the woman of his dreams, and he knew
it. From that day on we never parted. We had been
dating for nearly two years when on December 24, 2004
– my 23rd birthday – he decided it was time to take the
next logical step toward our lifelong future together.

We finished Christmas Eve dinner and opened gifts
at my parents' house, as was our annual tradition. But
then I broke tradition for the first time in my life when I
didn't spend the night in Paducah with my family. Josh
and I drove back to Murray instead. He said he wanted
to go back since we were going to spend time with his
family the next day. It was a 45-minute drive and it was
starting to snow, so it made sense to drive back there
that evening, but it also made me very sad.

Josh took me to my apartment and came in, but said he wanted to run a few doors down to see his friend for a minute. While he was gone, I went into my bedroom, called Mandy, and cried. I was so upset that I wasn't at home with them. I knew it was all part of growing up and that changes like that were going to happen, especially when in a serious relationship. But it was still difficult to swallow at that moment.

After being gone for a few minutes, Josh popped his head into my room and asked if I was alright. He could tell I was crying, but I told him I was fine. That seemed to be a good enough answer for him as he quickly left and closed the door. I continued to talk to Mandy for a few more minutes before hanging up. I wiped my eyes, regained my composure and opened the bedroom door to go out to the living room. I wheeled myself out there and…oh my!

All the lights were out and candles were lit throughout the room. My first thought was that he was doing something sweet for me on my birthday. And he was, but sweeter than I could have ever imagined. He turned on a CD. I don't have a clue what the song was. I know it wasn't our song "Amazed" by Lonestar, but it was something romantic. That's why he'd been at his friend's house. He had hoped his friend had our song, but he didn't, so Josh took whatever romantic tune he could find. And now I knew why it was so important to him to come back to Murray that night. Yeah, our Christmas Day plans with his family had something to do with it, but that wasn't the real reason.

He bent down on one knee and stared into my eyes.

"Missy, I love you so much and I want to take care of you forever," he said. "Will you marry me?" With that, he opened up a box with the most beautiful diamond ring! I was so excited that I couldn't even speak. I just grabbed him and hugged him with tears in my eyes.

"So will you?" he asked. I realized I hadn't given him an answer.

"YES!" I cried.

He wanted to surprise me, and he did. I had a feeling a ring might be coming soon, but it was just a feeling. I didn't know when, and I certainly didn't think it would be that evening. I couldn't have asked for a better birthday. We hugged. We kissed. I called Mandy again and was crying again, but this time, of course, they were happy tears. It was my birthday. It was Christmas Eve. And now it was the night I got engaged. As a line in our song says: "It just keeps getting better."

Josh and I knew we were meant to be together and that we wanted to spend the rest of our lives together. There was no doubt. We knew our love for each other was so strong that nothing could stand in our way. But we also knew that, before we got married, we needed to talk about some things: religion, intimacy, children, and how he would be able to handle living with a paraplegic. We needed to clearly understand each other and have no surprises down the road.

Josh and I were raised by our parents to have a deep faith in God, something that stuck with us into our adult lives and something we felt was very important to the foundation of our relationship. Knowing we both had strong morals based on God's commandments made it very easy to trust each other. And we knew that when we ran into any difficult times during our marriage, as all married couples do, we would have the love and respect for each other, along with God's grace, to help us get through them.

Our only real difference when it came to our faith was our denominations. I belonged to the Church of Christ. Josh was Methodist. While our religions had some differences, we were both Christians, and that's all that mattered to us. We decided that since we were going to live in Murray, we'd attend the church he grew up in. Anytime we were in Paducah on a Sunday morning, we'd go to my church. What was most important to us was that we simply go to church. It had a positive effect on our individual lives in so many ways, and we felt it was something we needed to continue to do together for the strength and health of our marriage.

Another aspect to a healthy marriage is intimacy. One question Josh had for me was "Being paralyzed, how 'intimate' can you be?" Well, to put it simply, I could do what any person who wasn't paralyzed could do. That intimacy may not physically feel the same to me as it might to someone who wasn't paralyzed. But I had nothing to compare it to. I had never been *that* close to a guy before the shooting, so I really couldn't say for sure. What I did know for sure was that we could be as intimate as we wanted to be, and it would not be a barrier in our relationship.

Another question related to that was whether or not the paralysis affected my ability to have children. I honestly didn't know and hadn't thought about it until he asked me. My guess was that I could have children because I knew there were paralyzed people in the world who did bear children. I asked a doctor to be certain, and she assured me that I could. The actual birth might be a bit unusual in the sense that I likely wouldn't feel any contractions or pain, but aside from that, everything would be normal.

The matter of living with a paralyzed person was actually not a concern at all to Josh. In fact, it was I who was worried about it. The biggest problem, in my mind, was the bathroom issue. Even though I told him about it while we were dating, and it never seemed to bother him, I wondered why a guy would want to be with a woman who had accidents on herself or had to plan her life around the bathroom. But he never looked at it as being a concern. To him it was just part of who I was and that was the end of it. He would always say to me, "It really doesn't matter to me. It's no big deal. You worry too much about it." Finally I decided one day that I simply had to trust him on that.

It was like after the shooting when I decided I wasn't going to get angry about it. Nobody could understand how I could feel that way, but they decided that since it didn't bother me, it shouldn't bother them. In this case, I finally decided that since it didn't bother Josh, it shouldn't bother me.

While I knew people close to me who had been married and then divorced, I didn't hesitate to commit the rest of my life to Josh. Our relationship wasn't something we just jumped into. We allowed it to evolve slowly and naturally over nearly two years. We'd each dated other people in college before meeting each other, but nobody made us feel like we did when we were with each other.

Our relationship worked from the start for a lot of reasons: we had a lot in common and both of us were mature people and always wanted to be together. The biggest key to our success, though, was communication. We had an open communication and knew we would never survive without it. Since we've been married, we've always made it a point to say "I love you," hug, and set aside time for each other every single day. It's unfortunate that we live in such a fast-paced world where spouses have to "schedule" time for each other, but if that's what it takes to make it work, then that's what should be done.

Yes, we knew there would be arguments like any other married couple has, but we felt we'd always be able to work our way through them with honest communication. We agreed we would never go to bed angry or leave for work angry. And if something so terrible ever did happen that we felt it could jeopardize our marriage, we agreed that we would seek counseling together immediately.

Marriage is very sacred to us. It's been sacred in both of our families for generations, and ending it before one of us dies simply was not an option to us. We decided from the start that we were in it forever. We were making that commitment to ourselves, our family, our future children, and to God. We knew that together we could do it. It was going to be a lot of hard work, but we didn't expect anything less for something we felt was so worthwhile.

18

THE REAL WORLD

Josh and I had graduated from Murray State six days before our engagement and were going full-steam ahead into the "real world" in 2005. We decided to continue living in town, and I started working in January as an elementary school substitute teacher in a western Kentucky public school district. I then subbed as a para-educator (teacher assistant) in that district's day treatment center before I was hired there full time in February as a para-educator and counselor.

The center served as many as 30 youth at a time, students who struggled to function in a mainstream classroom because of various issues: bad home lives, no respect for authority, mental health problems, violent tendencies, victims of bullying. They'd go there for a six-month program where we would work with them on their school work and personal issues in one-on-one and group sessions before returning them to their old school.

I was one of three counselors there when I was hired in February. In May, after one counselor left, I dropped the "para-educator" from my title and became one of two full-time counselors. Then in October our head counselor left, leaving me in charge – and alone. For the next three months, until another counselor was hired in January 2006, I was the only counselor to 25 kids. Looking back on it, I have no idea how I did it, especially considering I'd only been on the job for eight months. I had to do 25 individual counseling sessions each week, group sessions each day and a ton of paperwork on each child. It was very stressful, but I enjoyed the challenge of it – and still do. Today I'm the head counselor, and one of two counselors at the facility.

Like any job, mine has its ups and downs. The "up" moments are when a child listens to my advice, shows a willingness to change, and works on improving his or her life. The "down" moments are when, no matter what I do to try to help a student, there is simply no way to get through to him or her.

One thing I've learned in this profession is that I can't make anybody do anything. I can give them advice, but they have to want to change for it to work. The head counselor who left in October 2005 was the one who helped me realize that. He used to tell me I couldn't let it get to me if a student didn't take my advice or didn't turn out the way I had hoped, but that can be difficult. Not getting emotionally involved with students is a basic rule in this profession, but seeing a kid with so much potential and not reaching it is very frustrating.

My attitude toward each student who comes in is the same: I'm going to do everything within my power to make that child realize his or her potential, show that child how to change, and get him or her back into a mainstream school in six months without the worry that the child will ever have to come back to the center. But my attitude doesn't guarantee success. There have been many times when I think I've gotten through to someone but really haven't. I've seen kids come into my office because they did something they shouldn't have. But, after we talk, they walk out of the office and continue doing what they were just told not to do. I've asked myself so many times, "Was I just talking to this wall? Why is this so hard for them to grasp?" The reasons can be numerous, from a problem with a classmate to problems at home. And that's where the challenge comes in. Can I help this person change? Will this person allow me to help him or her change? Maybe. Maybe not. But I go in every time thinking "yes" to both of those questions, and give it my best shot.

I've had several success stories of students who have come in troubled and left better people. And even the simplest moments can be gratifying. I had one boy who had something stolen from him one day. He insisted that another boy he'd had problems with before had stolen it. He yelled at that boy and accused him of taking it, but he never had any proof. As it turned out, the boy he accused didn't take it, so he apologized – without me having to tell him to. He told the accused boy that he was sorry and that he was wrong to blame him. The boy who had been blamed told him to forget about it and it was over. Part of me couldn't believe what I'd witnessed, but it was proof that our counseling sessions had worked.

Another time two boys were playing in the gym. One boy threw a ball and hit the other one. The boy who was hit insisted it was done on purpose and was ready to fight the boy who threw it at him. They were separated and told to cool off. A little while later, after they'd calmed down, the boy who threw the ball went up to the boy he hit and told him he really didn't mean to do it and that he was sorry. As in the other case, they dropped it and that was that.

When I see moments like that, it's a good boost to my morale and helps justify my work. It reminds me that they do have ways they can cope; they just need to believe in what those of us are trying to instill in them.

Of course, not every case has a happy ending. I had one girl with whom I talked more than once each day about her anger and negative attitude about everything. She had numerous personal problems, but she just couldn't deal with them. No matter how hard I tried, I couldn't help her. In fact, one day when she was in my office, after I'd tried for weeks to help her out, she just said "I'm done. I quit." When they think that way, there's nothing that can be done. I can't change them. There has to be some effort on their part. Without it, there is little hope for improvement.

Do I feel like I've failed after dealing with someone like that? Sure I do. I don't let it get me down, though, at least not for too long. I always remind myself that I tried. As long as I know I did everything I could, I have to be satisfied with that. If I beat myself down every time I don't get through to a kid, I'd mentally drain myself. There would be no way I could continue in this line of work.

As tough as the job can be at times, I do what I do because of the shooting. Before that I had no idea what I wanted to do with my life. The shooting and aftermath made me realize that I could use my experiences to help kids. When I have a child I'm struggling with, I sometimes think of Michael and how he felt that he had nobody he could turn to. I think about how I need to keep reaching out, keep trying, and keep focused on the child until I've gotten through to him or her, or until I've exhausted every possible option.

I use the shooting experience to my advantage as much as I can. The kids are always curious about why I'm in a wheelchair, and they are shocked when I tell them how it happened. For a few, it's enough to scare them straight. For others, it goes in one ear and out the other. But I find that it has a positive effect on many of them. It helps me teach them about the consequences of violence, respecting peers and making the right choices.

They can look at me and see first-hand how their choices can have a lifelong impact on others. I tell them where Michael is today, and they can hear how their choices can have a lifelong impact on themselves. The key for me is to not only make them realize that while they're in my care, but to drill it into them enough that they never forget it. After they leave, our hope is that they never have to come back.

I love what I do and plan to continue counseling for many years, though I have given some thought to some other possibilities in the future. In the summer of 2005, four months into my job, I started law school at American Justice School of Law in Paducah. My initial thought was that it would be a backup plan if the counseling profession didn't work out but, since it has, I've stopped attending law school for the time being. I took some basic courses for a year, mainly in contract law and family law. I may return at some point, but I've decided instead to get my master's degree in social work since the counseling job is going so well. With all I have going on in my life, it may take me a few years to complete my master's program, but I intend to stick it out until that degree is in hand. Maybe I could use it to start my own practice one day. Who knows? What I do know for sure is that I love working with youth and trying to make a positive impact in their lives.

Also in the summer of 2005, Josh and I bought a house together and moved into it a year before we were married. We decided to do that to make sure we could tolerate each other, but we "lived together" in a different sense: we had separate bedrooms. Some people thought it was wrong that we lived together at all before marriage, even with separate bedrooms, but we felt it was important to see how compatible we were before committing to each other for the rest of our lives. As I said earlier, divorce was not an option to us. Once we made that commitment, it was golden. So why not do all we could to make sure marriage was meant for us?

I can honestly say it's something we've never regretted doing. We learned a lot about each other, such as our capabilities in managing a house and our quirky habits. I learned how to get around the house and what my limitations were (such as what cupboards I could and couldn't reach). Most importantly, it gave Josh an opportunity to adjust to living with someone with a disability. In our minds, by keeping separate bedrooms, we were able to stay true to our morals while learning more about each other. We were absolutely certain on our wedding day that we would be able to live together forever.

Josh and I made it official on June 24, 2006. We chose that day to get married because we wanted a summer wedding and because 24, simply by chance, had become a significant number. We were both 24 years old, met two years earlier on February 24th and were engaged on my birthday, December 24, 2004.

We married at First United Methodist Church in Murray. When I arrived that day, I met with my bridesmaids and got ready. But then I did something a little bit unconventional: I met with Josh. I know brides and grooms aren't supposed to see each other before the ceremony, but we chose to do so. Within the church was a small chapel where we met. Josh was sitting in the front pew when I wheeled myself in. He handed me a red rose and told me how beautiful I looked. We sat together and quietly talked and prayed for a while. It was a moment I'll never forget. It gave us an opportunity to get away from all the excitement and fanfare and place ourselves in a solemn state with a focus on God, the one who brought us together.

My bridesmaids were Mandy, Kelly, Taylor, Nora, and a woman I worked with named Becky Coggeshall. My dad walked down the aisle next to me as I wheeled myself down to the altar. I sat for most of the ceremony, but stood with the help of my brace and walker during our vows. It was absolutely wonderful to be able to look Josh straight in the eyes during that very special moment.

With the aid of my brace, I was able to stand and look Josh in the eyes during the first dance as husband and wife.
(Photo by Allison Photography, Murray, KY)

Our reception was at Murray Country Club and was attended by a few hundred people. I was able to stand again there and danced with Josh to our song, "Amazed." That night we stayed in our own home, then drove to Nashville, Tennessee, the next morning. From there we flew to Cancun, Mexico, for a week-long honeymoon.

Overall, my wedding day was everything I dreamt it would be. The weather was nice, the ceremony was exactly as I'd hoped, and the reception was just one big party with the people I loved. Looking back on it, I was so happy with the way Josh and I managed the early years of our relationship together. We got off to a slow start those first couple of times after we met, but we gave it a chance and it worked. We took our time, stuck to our principles, communicated with each other about everything, and worked hard to be sure that we were doing the right thing. We knew we still had a lot of work ahead of us, but we were ready for it, starting with a new addition to our family.

In September 2006, I went to my gynecologist and asked her some questions about the possibility of me having a child. I had asked before and knew that I could, but I just wanted to be sure that the baby and I would both be safe during the time I carried the baby and while giving birth. Josh and I had talked about having children after we got married and felt we were ready to be parents. With each of us having a stable job (he's a physical education teacher at a local middle school) and our own home, we felt it was time to try. The doctor reiterated that everything would be fine.

One day in January 2007, I was starting to feel nauseous. It continued for a few days, and I seemed to always be tired, even though I was getting plenty of sleep. I didn't think there was any way that I was pregnant already, but I bought a home pregnancy test to be sure. I took it and left it sitting on the bathroom sink counter. Josh then went into the bathroom and looked at it.

"Uh, Missy, there are two lines on this thing," he said with some hesitancy. The two lines meant the test was positive. I was stunned! I had no idea I would get pregnant so soon. In fact, I bought two more tests and took them each of the next two days. Same results! I went to the doctor that week, and she confirmed that we were going to have a baby in September.

Anyone who has had a baby knows what that feeling is like when you find out you're pregnant for the first time. It's elation and nervousness at the same time. You think of everything from, "What should I be doing or eating right now?" to "What color will we paint the nursery?" There's no feeling like it in the world.

We had so many other questions we had to answer: "What would we name the baby? Would I continue working after the baby was born? How would I, as a paraplegic, be able to take care of the baby? Was there a crib that could safely be low enough to the ground so I could pick up the baby out of it and lay the baby back into the crib? Was there a changing table that could be at my level? How would I give the baby a bath? How would I get the baby in and out of the car?"

Of course, I knew Josh would have to be the greatest husband and dad in the world and help out more than the spouse of someone who was not disabled might have to, and I had no doubt that he would. But I also knew I wouldn't be the first paraplegic to have a child. I talked with one woman I met in the Miss Wheelchair Kentucky pageant who was a paraplegic with children. While she gave me advice on some of the tricks of the trade, just knowing that she was able to do it was enough to tell me I could do it, too. Was I scared? Sure I was. I knew it wouldn't be easy, but it could be done. The way I saw it, I had faced and conquered every challenge thrown at me up to that point in my life. There was no reason to believe that I couldn't conquer motherhood.

To help myself prepare, I searched some web sites for disabled parents that gave me some ideas of what we could do to help me with the physical demands of parenting. For example, we could modify a crib so that it could open from the side at my level. That way I wouldn't have to worry about hoisting the baby over the top.

As for lifting the baby, that would all depend on my physical strength. I had always had a strong upper body because of all the physical therapy and weight lifting I'd done over the years. I knew that was something that I would have to keep doing so that my strength would grow with the baby's weight. I figured the most difficult thing I would probably have to do would be to get the baby in and out of the car. A lot of that would depend on my strength to lift the carrier and baby into the back seat. But that would be just the beginning. After that, I'd have to buckle the baby in and then get myself in. Then I'd have to pull the wheels off my wheelchair as I do now but, instead of tossing the wheels and seat into the back seat, I'd have to buckle it all in the front seat so that if there were ever an accident, the pieces of the chair wouldn't fly around the car and be a danger to the baby. And then what would happen when I got us all in and realized I'd left the diaper bag in the house? Ugh! I didn't even want to think about that.

As excited as I was to be a mom, some people told me that if there was anything I wanted to do before giving birth, I should do it because my life would change drastically once the baby arrived. In other words, my baby would become my overwhelming focus. I would see my friends less. Vacations would be limited. Projects around the house would be pushed into the future again and again. Even something as simple as going out to dinner would become less frequent. I was OK with all of that.

To me, part of the responsibility of being a parent was to reorganize my priorities, realizing that the baby's needs always come first. But I did heed that advice and give some serious thought to what I might want to do before the baby was born. Strangely enough, taking trips or doing any other fun things weren't at the top of my list. What was at the top were two issues related to the shooting.

The first thing I wanted to do was spend some time learning more about Michael's appeal. He had appealed his case three years earlier and it was still pending, but I knew very little about it. I noticed it had been making headlines recently, and I really didn't know why. Could he get out of prison or at least get a lesser sentence, as some people had suggested to me? It seemed like the case was starting to get more attention from the courts. I wanted to spend some time reading about it, figuring out what the truth was and ridding myself of any potential stress from it.

I know to some people that may not sound like something that had to be done before the baby was born or something that would take a lot of time, but it was a big deal to me to get it out of the way. And whether it took me a day or a week or a month to get the answers I wanted, the point was that I needed to make sure I got it done. I knew I'd be under a lot of stress once I became a mother. The last thing I wanted was to be blindsided by a subpoena that would force me to testify at a trial involving his appeal. It was just something I needed to be prepared for.

The second thing I wanted to do was something I had talked about since 2006 – meet with Michael. When I told some people I wanted to do that, they told me I was crazy. Many thought he might hurt me more. Some thought it would appear that I was being too sympathetic if I were to meet with him. But I had too many unanswered questions about that tragic day – questions that only he could answer. If I could meet with him before my baby's birth, I felt that it would lift a huge weight off my shoulders. Even if he didn't give me the answers I was seeking, at least I could say I tried. I figured either way I would leave with a better understanding of who he was. That, to me, was worth the chance.

19

MICHAEL'S APPEAL

Michael's appeal was officially initiated by Michael and his attorneys from the state department of public advocacy on June 1, 2004, his 21st birthday. That was when he filed paperwork to move "for relief from his judgment on the ground that his schizophrenia rendered him incompetent in October 1998 to plead guilty." He claimed more than six years after the shooting that he was, in fact, schizophrenic when he entered his "guilty, but mentally ill" plea in October 1998 and, therefore, was not competent to enter such a plea. He wanted it thrown out, which could then result in him changing his plea and his case going to trial.

Fortunately it took Judge Hines, the one who sentenced Michael in 1998, just 30 days to find that Michael's motion was untimely and refuted by the record. That made sense to me. Michael waited more than six years to make his claim and was not considered to be schizophrenic in 1998 by any of the doctors who evaluated him.[54] But Hines' ruling wasn't the end of it. After Hines dismissed the claim, Michael took his case to the Kentucky Court of Appeals. At 10 A.M. on May 26,

2006, the judges on that court vacated Hines' order and sided with Michael.

I'm not going to talk about this in great length because it's still pending, and I don't think it's very productive for me to get into the intricate details of something that could drag on for many years. But I do want to address how the Court of Appeals came to that decision and what it could mean for the families of the girls who died, the other five of us who were shot, and the rest of the people in Paducah who are still healing today.

The May 26, 2006 published opinion by the Court of Appeals states the following background information:

> "Because an insanity defense was not supported even by his own experts, Carneal and his parents agreed to a guilty plea. They did so not in exchange for a bargain from the Commonwealth, but rather because Carneal felt he deserved the maximum punishment; because all of them wished to spare him, his victims, and his victims' families the ordeal of a trial; and because they sought treatment for his mental problems as quickly as possible."[55]

Sounds logical and simple enough. He shot us, felt he deserved the maximum punishment, spared us a trial and needed help. I wish all offenders took that road. But is the court system ever that black and white? Here's what the Court of Appeals wrote after that:

> "Carneal alleges in his current motion that some time after his transfer to adult custody in June 2001, he began to be treated with the antipsychotic medications Geodon and Zyprexa. Under this treatment he gradually attained a degree of detachment from an elaborate system of auditory and visual hallucinations and of paranoid fears and ideations that he had begun to experience about six months before the shootings and of which the shootings formed a part. Prior to this treatment, he claims, he experienced voices warning him not to reveal anything about his delusional system.

As a result, he told his examiners in 1998 and his doctors since then very little about it. Only recently has he gained the ability to hold his delusions somewhat at bay and to discuss them with others. He has since been reexamined by Drs. Cornell and Schetky (the doctors who evaluated him on his behalf in 1998) and has attached their reevaluations of his condition to his motion for relief. Both doctors find Carneal's revelations credible and both state that had Carneal been forthcoming in 1998 about the extent of his delusional involvement they would have deemed him insane at the time of the offense. Dr. Cornell, furthermore, the only expert in 1998 asked to assess Carneal's competence for trial, would now opine that Carneal was not competent."[56]

In other words he now claims that when he was being evaluated in 1998, voices in his head told him not to tell anybody that he was insane. But then he started taking medication in prison and those voices began to subside. That led the doctors, who in 1998 claimed that he was competent to enter his guilty plea, to now say that he was actually not competent to enter that plea.

The Court of Appeals stated in its opinion that Michael should receive a retrospective competency hearing, if such a hearing would be practicable after all of these years. They concluded by saying:

"If a retrospective competency determination is not feasible, or if it is determined at the hearing that Carneal was not competent to enter his guilty plea, then he shall be permitted to withdraw the plea and, if competent to do so, either plead again, or proceed to trial."[57]

I can't say I'm surprised that Michael and his attorneys have done this. How many times do prisoners appeal their cases? It seems that they all do. Michael is sitting in prison with nothing to do and absolutely nothing to lose. How much lower can life get for him?

But despite his right to do this, it's still very sad, disappointing, and frustrating to me that Michael, his attorneys, and his family are going through with it. I agree that no matter what his diagnosis was or is, he needs to get treatment for it. But he should not be doing anything that is going to open the wounds he inflicted on the people he's already hurt.

What happened to his agreement of life in prison without the chance of parole for 25 years because he felt he deserved the maximum punishment? And what happened to the fact that "all of them wished to spare him, his victims, and his victims' families the ordeal of a trial?" Do they no longer care about putting the Stegers, Jameses, Hadleys, Jenkinses, Holms, Schabergs, Keenes, and Hards through all that? Because that's exactly what would happen if he gets a trial more than a decade later. I realize those close to Michael are concerned about his health, but how they can live with putting us all through more pain for his benefit is beyond me.

What's also at stake here is that if he were able to change his plea to "not guilty by reason of insanity" and a judge or jury agreed, he could be moved from the prison he's in today to a mental hospital and be discharged when he's deemed to no longer be a threat. That could be never, or it could be any time. I want him to be able to get the help he needs, but there has to be a way to receive help without him being released from prison. And if he can't get the help he feels he needs in prison, then his energy should be focused on changing that so that he and people like him can get the help they need while behind bars. Putting us through more pain to benefit himself should not be an option for him in my opinion.

So where does the case stand as of this writing? After the Court of Appeals sided with Michael, it was up to the Kentucky Supreme Court to decide if it wanted to review the case or not. If the court decided not to review it, the Court of Appeals ruling would have stood and Michael would have been much closer to getting the trial he wanted. But thankfully, on March 14, 2007, the Supreme Court decided to begin reviewing the case.[58] In early 2008, both sides filed briefs, and oral arguments were expected to begin in September 2008. Some attorneys told me that it would likely be very late in 2008, or even 2009, before a decision is rendered. We can only pray that the justices side with the victims, but who knows what will happen.

What I do know is that it's out of my control, so I try not to think about it much. No matter what the state Supreme Court rules, there will probably be more appeals from one side or the other, which could push a possible trial well into the next decade. So I don't think it's very good use of my time or energy to worry about it at this point. I can't let what he's doing affect my daily life. Like I've done ever since the day of the shooting, I need to focus on my faith in God, my recovery, and all the wonderful people in my life. I also need to continue teaching people everything I can from my experiences. That's why I initiated the second issue that I mentioned earlier: meeting with Michael.

When I've talked to children about my experiences, I've oftentimes gotten a lot of questions from them about Michael: "Why did he do it? Has he changed for the better since that day? Is he sorry for what he did?" Some questions I've tried to answer, but often I couldn't because I had never spoken with him about them. While I've frequently received ovations for the talks I've given and people have seemed to walk away from them having learned something, the inability for me to answer those questions about Michael for the audience has always nagged at me. I decided, for my benefit and for the benefit of those I talk to, I needed to close that gap.

And so at 1:30 P.M on July 21, 2007, after years of thinking about it and months of planning with some of

Michael's representatives, Mandy and I made the 250-mile drive to La Grange, Kentucky. We had an appointment to meet face to face with Michael Carneal.

20

My Visit with Michael

The process of meeting with Michael actually began in November 2006. A friend of mine helped me with it by contacting someone he knew in the Kentucky Department of Corrections to see if such a visit would even be possible. The department didn't oppose the idea but seemed to be nervous about it given the fact that it was such a rare request for them to receive and because they didn't have a lot of experience in dealing with such a request. We went back and forth for a few months, trying to make it work, but didn't get very far.

We got some new life, though, in March, when I received a call from a representative with the *Oprah Winfrey Show*. She said Oprah was doing a show on forgiveness and they were considering me as a guest. They wanted to get Michael and me together and tape our meeting so they could air it. Ironically, they had no idea that I had already been working on trying to visit with him. I wasn't opposed to a meeting being on camera, if that's what it was going to take to make it happen. In the end, though, Oprah's request was declined by Michael's attorneys. I did, however, get the

impression that his attorneys weren't necessarily
opposed to Michael and me getting together privately.
While an appearance on *Oprah* didn't work out, I figured
it couldn't hurt to contact Michael's attorneys directly
and see if we could negotiate something.

When I contacted them, they said they would ask
Michael and get back with me as soon as they could. So
I waited. And waited. And waited. About four weeks
later, on April 19, an email from them arrived indicating
Michael was interested in visiting with me. However,
due to the shootings at Virginia Tech just a few days
earlier, they felt waiting at least a couple months would
be best to assure Michael's stability. I was fine with that.
What mattered to me was that it appeared this meeting
might actually happen.

To go ahead, though, I needed more than just the
approval of Michael and his lawyers. The commissioner
of the corrections department and the prison warden
also had to be on board. The warden told Michael's
attorneys that he wasn't against the idea, but the warden
wanted us to get a facilitator – someone trained in
victim/offender visits who could mediate such a meeting
and assure the warden and commissioner that the
meeting would be a good thing for all parties involved.

Michael's attorneys and I hired Linda Harvey of
Restorative Associates in Lexington. She had an impres-
sive resume that included bringing together several
prisoners convicted of homicide with the families of the
people they killed. She also included another mediator,
Jeff From, in the process.

The plan was for the meeting to include Linda, Jeff,
Mandy, Michael, Kelly (Michael's sister), and me.
Michael's attorneys did not want any attorneys from
either side present in the room because they felt that
could only hinder the possibility of a fruitful discussion
taking place. I talked to my attorney and he didn't see
anything wrong with that given that I had already

publicly forgiven Michael, and it wasn't like I was going to go in there to beg for the prison to release him.

The process started in early July with Linda and Jeff meeting once with Michael, once with Mandy and me, and once with Kelly. The meetings, each an hour or two long, took place over the course of about a week with the goal of making sure we were all ready for this. We were asked what happened the day of the shooting from each of our perspectives, what we wanted to get out of the meeting, and how we felt toward each other. After talking with all of us, Linda said she had no doubt we were all ready. She said Michael was looking forward to seeing me and that he would answer any questions I asked and listen to whatever I wanted to say. I was also looking forward to seeing his sister, Kelly. Though I didn't really know her that well at Heath, I knew what a good person she was and that having her there could only help the situation.

Linda scheduled the meeting for July 21 at the reformatory in La Grange, where Michael had been since he turned 18 six years prior. That's when it really hit me that this was going to actually happen. For the first time, I became very nervous. I really wasn't that nervous for me as I knew I could handle it. It's what I wanted. But I was nervous for my baby. Would the stress be too much? Could my baby's health be in any danger? I gave it a lot of thought, talked with Linda about it a little more, and finally decided everything would be fine. Many people had put forth a lot of effort to make this happen, and there was no guarantee that I would ever get this chance again. I knew deep down that there wouldn't be any problems. If I got there and felt like I couldn't do it, I could simply turn around and leave. But at least I had to make the effort.

On July 20, I drove from my home in Murray to Paducah and spent the night at my parents' house with Mandy. The next morning we headed for La Grange to meet face to face with the person who changed my life forever nearly 10 years earlier.

We arrived in La Grange at about 12:45 P.M. and went to Michael's attorneys' office at the Department of Public Advocacy where we met with David Harshaw (one of Michael's attorneys), Linda, Jeff, and Kelly. Linda went over a few things with us, then we all headed to the prison. As we left the office, Mandy and I were chatting away with Kelly like old friends, reminiscing about Paducah and people we knew at Heath. She looked great and seemed very happy. I found out that she visited Michael every week, something I really admired about her. I can't imagine the hell she went through in the years after the shooting. I felt that she, too, was a victim of that tragedy. Yet she stuck by her brother – certainly not because she condoned what he did, but because he was her brother. My guess is that her presence and love have done Michael a lot of good over the years.

We each drove our own cars to the prison. Mandy and I were at the end of the four- or five-car motorcade. We weren't going much more than 25 miles per hour on some country roads that were completely foreign to us. Part of me was glad that we were taking our time, but another part of me was anxious to get there. Each time we turned a corner, we nervously looked to see if we were there yet. Then, after driving for about five minutes, we looked to our right and there it was. It had to be at least a third of a mile off the road: a tall, narrow tower, probably 10 or 12 stories high, flanked by a wing of the prison on either side and surrounded by barbed wire.

My heart raced as we made what was probably a 20-second drive into the complex, though it felt more like several minutes. The driveway seemed to go on and on and on. Here I was, voluntarily entering the grounds where 2,000 murderers, sex offenders, and every other type of criminal resided. And one of those murderers was inside waiting for me. Did I really want to do this?

When we reached the parking lot, I turned off the car and took several deep breaths. I was fine, I told myself. This was it. This is what I wanted. It was time.

We first checked in with identification at a security gate outside. We then went through the front iron gates of the 71-year-old facility. One officer checked our identifications again while another ran a wand around us to make sure we weren't bringing anything in from outside. We were met by Paige McGuire, the deputy warden at the prison who was kind enough to come in on her day off to organize the meeting and make sure we had what we needed.

She led us a short distance to a room where parole hearings are generally held, but the door to the room was locked and she didn't have the correct key. We waited anxiously for a minute while she went to get it. When she got back, she unlocked it and opened the door. I really didn't know what to expect. I guess I figured I'd wheel myself in, get comfortable, and then Michael would be led in with handcuffs and shackles. But that's not at all what happened.

I entered the room and found Michael waiting there for us. Tan jumpsuit. No handcuffs. No shackles. He was standing on one side of a long table. My heart was racing faster than when we had arrived on the prison grounds. I wasn't feeling sick. I didn't want to leave. I was just nervous. Very nervous.

Michael was tall, medium build, wearing thick glasses and, quite frankly, reminded me of the Michael Carneal I knew in school, just an older version. I took a deep breath and said hello with a smile, mainly to try to break the tension inside my own body and mind. He was looking at the floor, but looked up long enough to say hello back. He sat down while Mandy and I sat on the opposite side of the table. Kelly went around and sat next to her brother. Linda and Jeff sat at the head of the table, to my left. We all signed a few legal documents and were ready to go. I had two hours to say what I wanted to say and to listen to what he had to say. I was still nervous, but ready. My opportunity had arrived.

We made a deal with Michael and his attorneys before the meeting that it would be audio taped, and that I would get a copy of the transcript. The transcript was never to be shown to anyone. However, I could quote anything that I said and paraphrase anything that Michael said during our discussion when giving my talks or writing my book. After all, the primary reason for me wanting to have this meeting was to be able to try to help those people I speak to by giving them some answers that only Michael could answer.

The meeting was scheduled to last for two hours. Nobody really knew if Michael would make it that long, but he was willing to try. I was told that he didn't have a very long attention span and might get restless, needing breaks every 20 minutes or so. Whatever it took for him to be able to carry on a conversation with me was fine with me.

Linda had organized the meeting in a way that Mandy and I would say what we wanted and ask Michael any questions we wanted. Then he would get to do the same to us, as would Kelly. But because we were all so comfortable with each other, it pretty much turned into a free-for-all conversation. Mandy and I definitely did most of the talking, but everybody seemed pleased with the casualness of it all.

Aside from looking at me briefly to say hello when I entered the room, Michael's focus was straight down at the floor. I thought that maybe he felt like he shouldn't look at me because of what he'd done to me. It reminded me of when he kept his head down during the sentencing. Part of me wanted to tell him to look at me, as I told him to do during the sentencing, but a bigger part of me wanted him to do it on his own this time. Anything that he did during this visit, I wanted it to be because it was what he wanted to do, not because it was what I wanted him to do.

As soon as we started our dialogue, he lifted his head up and suddenly seemed to realize that it was OK to look at me. That's when my heart rate slowed down to normal and everything seemed fine for both of us. That initial tension that I think we both expected had subsided. We continued to keep eye contact throughout the conversation. Instead of focusing on the mere presence of each other, we each focused on what the other was saying. That's exactly what I wanted.

I started the meeting with a very basic question: "Why did you agree to meet with me?" He said he felt that it was something he owed me, and that it was something that would emotionally be good for all of us. I couldn't have agreed more. I really did feel that he owed me the opportunity, but at the same time, I didn't want that to be his only reason to meet with me. I wanted him to want to do it, and I truly believed that day that he did. We were off to a good start.

I made it clear to him that Mandy and I both really cared for him back in high school. "Both of us, we've always liked you and we always thought you were a funny, hilarious, wonderful guy and we just, we wanted you to know that." He responded simply by thanking us. Throughout the entire conversation, Michael was often very short on words. Sometimes he would talk for a while and elaborate on certain topics, but a lot of times he just acknowledged what we said with a word or two, or a brief sentence. But as long as he answered my questions and heard what I said, that's all that mattered to me.

I moved on to the day of the shooting and asked him what he remembered. He said he remembered very little and, because so many people told him so many things about that day over the years, he didn't know if some of the events were truly his memories or just what others had said. So Mandy and I decided to tell him what happened from our perspective.

We told him where we were standing when he fired the shots, what we heard, what we saw, and what we felt. I talked about my rehabilitation, including the several months I spent in the hospital right after the shooting; my first trip to the movies in a wheelchair, when people kept bumping into me; wetting my pants when I returned to school, one of the most embarrassing moments of my life; the cathing I have to do; the trouble I had with dating after I was paralyzed; and the fact that, because of what he did to me, I couldn't feel my baby kicking in my womb.

I didn't show any emotion or try to make him feel bad as I told him those things. I simply wanted him to understand what he did to me and that, 10 years later, I was still affected by his actions. Throughout this part of the conversation, Michael hardly said a word, but I know he was listening. He stared straight into my eyes and nodded as I talked and talked and talked. He didn't cry, but he did tear up a little bit. It was the only emotion he showed throughout our talk, and it couldn't have come, at least from my perspective, at a more appropriate time.

I wanted him to know what we went through and wanted him to be able to somehow relate what he did that day to us today. I wanted him to feel the emotions we went through and understand how much he affected our lives. I wanted him to know that I was a 15-year-old girl lying on the ground, unable to move and unsure of whether I was going to live or die, all because of him. He heard me. I have no doubt. He heard me.

We talked about the six letters he wrote to me in 1999. He remembered that he had sent them but couldn't remember what he said in them. I told him that the timing of those letters just wasn't right. "I was graduating from high school. I was in L.A. learning how to use a brace to walk…I was doing a whole lot for myself," I said. "At that time I was just like, 'I can't. I can't do this right now.'"

He said that once I asked that his letters be stopped, he got into trouble. He was in a juvenile facility at the time and was on level three of four levels of good behavior. But once the jail found out he'd been writing to me, they dropped him to level one and made him do some cleaning around the facility with a toothbrush. He said that's why he never tried contacting me after that. As happy as I was that the letters stopped, I never intended for him to get in trouble. I think it's silly that they treated him that way over something that wasn't necessarily wrong of him to do – not very smart, but not wrong. But I guess it's one example of how life behind bars is a completely different world.

I shifted the conversation back to that tragic day to see if I could draw more out of him than I did earlier on what he remembered. "Do you remember your intentions that morning?" I asked him, hoping that rephrasing the earlier question would help. This time he seemed to remember some things. Maybe it was because he was more comfortable talking with me at this point in the conversation. Maybe it was because I had told the story from my perspective and it jogged his memory. Whatever the reason, he started talking more about that day.

He said that something inside him told him he needed to carry out the shooting. He didn't know what it was or why, but he just felt it was something he needed to do. And, as I expected, he didn't think of the consequences. He figured he would go to jail, he said, but the lives he might ruin never seemed to enter his mind. He couldn't explain why, but they just never did. He also recalled that the reason he put the gun down after shooting eight people was that he noticed a chip on a wall in the distance. He didn't say that he thought it was from one of the bullets, but that's what I assumed he was trying to say. After noticing the chip, he said he asked himself what he was doing and put the gun down, almost like seeing that chip woke him up from whatever world he was in.

He recalled being taken into the office by Mr. Bond and later interrogated by the detective. He also remembered being in court for his arraignment, and that when he was told he was being charged with three counts of murder, he said he had no idea whom he had killed. He said the entire experience just didn't seem real to him.

I asked him why he did it, and if it was because he was bullied. He said there was really no easy answer. Bullying may have been a part of it, he said. He told me several stories of him being bullied at school that I didn't know about, including a time he was hit in the kidneys and was urinating blood, and another time when a boy asked him for a doughnut, only to spit on it and give it back to him.

There was no doubt in my mind, after hearing his stories, that bullying played a factor in the shooting. He also admitted that he was the type of kid who kept his feelings inside and never told others if anything was bothering him, which certainly didn't help him deal with the abuse he took from other kids. He said he's since learned in prison that if he has a problem, he needs to tell somebody and not keep it bottled up.

He also pointed to his mental illness as a reason for what he did. He said he used to think that there was a group of people living in his house trying to kill him, and that he even saw glowing eyes in the vents of his house staring at him. He said he used to throw towels over the vents just to keep them away. And, eventually, he felt everybody around him could possibly be a member of that group.

I really didn't know what to make of that story. Thinking people are living in your house trying to kill you and reacting the way he did just seemed like such a big thing. How can someone keep something like that hidden? How did his family never notice it? How did he hide it from his friends and the kids at school? It just seemed so far fetched. I never noticed anything mentally wrong with him, but I can't say that I was around him enough that I would have noticed. And because I'm not him, I can never say for sure what his state of mind was.

I asked him if he felt he deserved to be in the prison. He said he knew he deserved to be punished, but he didn't really give me a direct answer. He talked about all the different opinions people have had. When he was transferred to La Grange from the juvenile detention center in Crittenden, he said one staff member greeted him by telling him that he should have been electrocuted. I think Michael understood why some people think that way, but he said he also believes treatment is an option. He then asked me what I thought.

Well, I certainly agree that treatment is a better option than death, but I also told him there are consequences for his actions and he needed to accept those consequences. What I found interesting throughout the two hours we were together was that he and I were carrying on a very normal conversation, just as any two people would. They said he may need to stop and take breaks, but he never needed to. His psychologist was on call in case he needed her at any point during our visit, but he never did.

While his appeal could get him out of prison and into a hospital, I really didn't see the need for that. Whatever medical treatment he's getting in the prison appeared to be working, at least that day. While I agree that he shouldn't be put to death for what he did, I do believe that staying behind bars in La Grange and continuing to receive the treatment he's receiving is a good option.

As our conversation wound down, we talked briefly about three more topics.

The first was about potential future contact. Linda asked us both if we would like to communicate with each other down the road. I was quick to answer: "Yeah, that would be fine," and Michael was also OK with it. I know back in 1999 I made him stop trying to contact me. But things were different now. The biggest difference was that I was now 25, not 17. Trying to deal with him writing to me while I was a teenager, and so soon after the shooting, was too much. But I felt now, especially after meeting with him, that I could handle it. I told him that I was a bit of a procrastinator and that he shouldn't expect any replies from me in a very timely manner, but if he wrote to me, I'd try to eventually write back.

My intent wasn't to be friends or even pen pals. My thought was that it would be another way for me to deal with what he did to me. It would be another form of therapy, a way for me not to just express my feelings, but to express them directly to him. I also left the door open for possible future visits. Honestly, I don't know that I'll ever need or want to visit him again. It's not something I'm planning on doing. But if I felt I needed to, at least that opportunity would be there. Or if a friend of mine who also knew Michael wanted to visit him and Michael was OK with it, it might be good for me to go since it's something I now have experience in doing.

The second topic was whether or not there was anything he would like me to tell people through the talks that I give. He had two simple responses: talk to somebody if you're having problems, and understand how much a kind word can mean to someone. Hearing him make those two points had such an impact on me, and I hope they mean something to the people I share them with. One has to wonder: if Michael had shared his problems with someone, and if the kids at school who picked on him used their energy to say kind things instead, would he have ever done what he did? We'll never know, but it's hard to imagine him feeling like he would have had any reason to carry out the shooting.

The final topic was brief and kind of came out of nowhere: an apology from him to Mandy and me. I didn't necessarily expect one, nor did I try to get him to think about it or say it. It just kind of happened. We were talking about my wheelchair and the various stories I had about it (like learning to do wheelies, and the time I fell backward in it before the Miss Wheelchair Kentucky pageant). He then started talking about people in prison who have wheelchairs and how every time he saw someone in one, it would make him think of me. He said it made him feel bad.

He then said he was sorry for what he had done to us. I told him he apologized several times in the letters he sent me and that I accepted every one of them back then. He was glad to hear that. But I will say that it was nice to hear him say it to me in person. It didn't change anything about my condition. It didn't bring back Jessica, Kayce, or Nicole. But it was pretty much all he could offer, and I felt that it was sincere.

I went into our meeting with few expectations, which is probably why I came out feeling so good about it. Kelly didn't say a whole lot throughout the meeting, but I think her intent was to be there simply to support not only her brother, but Mandy and me. Given how well our conversation was going, I don't think she wanted to interrupt that flow. She handled herself with class, and I appreciated her being there.

Mandy shared some stories throughout the conversation about our lives the past 10 years, but pretty much left the questioning up to me. There's been very little I've done in my life without her by my side, and there's no way I could have visited him without her next to me. For Linda and Jeff, I'm guessing this might have been the least stressful mediation either has ever been through. They were there to facilitate the discussion when necessary, but for the most part, they just sat back and let us go. They handled it well, and I'm glad they were able to be a part of it.

As for Michael, I hope he got something out of the visit. The fact that he didn't need to take any breaks, and he didn't need his psychologist when it was over were probably good signs for him. I hope he went back to his cell feeling that he did the right thing by meeting with me. It takes courage to face someone you've hurt, especially when that someone intends to share your conversation with the world. It's not something he had to do, but I'm very glad he did.

And as for me, I may not have received answers to everything, but I felt like I left the prison knowing more about him now and his thoughts the day of the shooting than I did before I went for the visit. What I got more than anything was confirmation about some of my theories: that the bullying had an impact on him; that he wasn't aiming for me or any of the others he shot; that he never thought of the consequences of his actions; and that he was sincerely sorry for what he did.

While it was sad to see him behind bars, it didn't change any of my feelings toward his situation. I still believe he needs to be where he is and serve out his life sentence. I've been saying for years that I will be at every parole board hearing he has to make sure that he never gets out, and I still feel that way. When people make decisions like the one he made that fateful day, they need to pay their debt to society. He was told at his sentencing that he could be eligible for parole in 25 years. But Jessica, Kayce, and Nicole will not be back then. I will likely not be walking then. So I don't see any reason why his sentence should be lessened.

The final point I want to make is that I hope people understand why I made this visit. As I said many chapters ago, people heal in different ways. I wouldn't necessarily expect the families of one of the girls he killed to want to meet with him. It may only hurt them more than it could help.

But for me, it was an opportunity to express my feelings directly to him. It was a chance for me to remind him what I look like in my wheelchair, something he hadn't seen since he saw me briefly at the sentencing. It was a chance for me to try to understand who Michael Carneal was, and is. It was a chance for me to show him my baby kicking inside of me, then tell him that while we could all see it, I couldn't feel it. It was a chance for me to try to get some answers for the kids I speak to who want to know more about him and why he did what he did. It was a chance for me to see him show a little emotion as I told him what he did to me that day. It was a chance for me to hear him say he was sorry.

I've always said that there will never be closure for me. But I think that visit was the closest I'll ever come.

21

My Life, My Destination

I've tried my best since the shooting to help people improve their lives and the world around them by sharing my experiences with them, and I know I've been successful in getting through to some of them. I've had two teenage students come to me at two separate talks I've given at schools in recent years and tell me that they had contemplated suicide but decided not to go through with it after hearing my story. They said I made them realize that, compared to what I and the others at Heath had gone through that day, their problems weren't so bad and that there are positive alternatives to help them deal with their tribulations. Stories such as those keep me going and make me realize that what I'm doing is worthwhile.

But aside from comparing what they're going through to what I've been through, there's so much more that I hope people learn from me:

- never assume that what you have today, from the use of your legs to your loved ones, will be here tomorrow;
- live a day at a time, and to the absolute fullest;

- make smart decisions that will not only positively impact you, but also those around you;
- don't ever think there is something you can't do;
- if you're running out of the house for school or work because you're late, make sure you take a couple seconds to tell your parents or spouse or children that you love them, just in case you never see them again;
- realize what's important in life, such as God, relationships, and an education;
- reach out to those who need help;
- don't bully people;
- say something nice to someone, just because;
- make the best of every situation;
- tell someone your problems rather than keeping them bottled up;
- enjoy the moment while keeping tomorrow in the back of your mind;
- choose happiness over anger;
and the list goes on and on.

But when I consider everything on that list, there are three lessons that really stand out to me above all the others that I hope people will always remember after hearing me talk or reading my story.

The first is that everything happens for a reason.

I think if we don't realize that, then we have a much more difficult time forgiving, recovering or doing whatever it is that we need to do to move forward with our lives in a positive way. By believing that God has a plan for us and that everything that happens to us is part of that plan, the door is opened for us to figure out what that reason is and to focus on what we can do to make things right or better again.

If I hadn't believed in that concept after I was shot, where would I be today? Still lying in bed feeling sorry for myself with no husband, no job, in poor health, and angry at the world? Quite possibly. But by believing there was a purpose for the shooting, I was able to forgive Michael, rehabilitate myself, and dedicate my life through my job and speeches and a book to helping other people overcome their adversities. I was able to come out of my shell and discover who I really was: a strong, confident, positive person with so many talents and abilities I never knew I had that could be shared with others.

People have asked if I would turn back time, if I could, so that I would have never been paralyzed. My answer is and always has been the same: if it would bring back Jessica, Kayce, and Nicole, then yes; but if we're talking about turning back time just for my sake, then no. Some people have a hard time comprehending that. They say that they don't understand how I could not want the use of my legs. Of course I would love to walk again. But the main purpose of my life since the shooting has never been about me being able to walk again.

I was given a second chance to live, and I believe the reason was, and is, to positively impact the lives of others through my disability. Considering the many lives I've affected in a positive way to this point, it would be selfish and irresponsible of me to wish that I had my old life back simply so I could walk. No way would I have made the contributions that I've made to the world if the shooting hadn't happened. That's why I'm leading the life that I'm leading and will continue to lead as long as I live.

How long that will be is a question I'm sometimes asked. Given that I'm a paraplegic, will that knock some years off my life? I truly don't know. I've never asked a doctor and don't really see the point in asking. I have heard some people say they've found on the Internet that, given the age at which I was paralyzed, I will likely live until I'm 60 or 65. I could see that being true. Because of my cathing, I've had several bladder infections and will likely have several more. How much can a bladder take?

My legs are much more susceptible to blood clots than those of an able-bodied person because I can't move them on my own. But whatever happens, happens. I take good care of myself. I eat well. I go to physical therapy a couple times a week. When I'm sick, I see a doctor. There's not much more I can do, other than rely on my faith and believe that God will never give me more than I can handle.

Everything happens for a reason. Whatever God's plan is for me – I accept it.

The second lesson is that forgiveness is a powerful thing.

I received some letters in 2007 from some seventh grade students at St. Joseph School in Crescent Springs, Kentucky, who had heard about my story. They said how amazed they were that I was able to forgive Michael so quickly. Some couldn't believe that I could forgive him at all. But the common theme throughout the letters was that they found it so much easier to forgive their brothers or sisters or friends because I was able to forgive, and that their lives are better because of it.

After the tragic shootings at Virginia Tech University in 2007 that took 33 lives, I read about one girl who was killed who had written some of her favorite quotes in a notebook that her father found in her dorm room. She wrote: "When a deep injury is done to us, we never recover until we forgive...Forgiveness does not change the past, but it does enlarge the future."[57]

I couldn't have said it any better. I will never forget what Michael did to me. How can I? I'm reminded of it every day when I can't jump out of bed in the morning, reach the cabinets in our kitchen, or stand face to face with my husband. There will never be closure. I will be living the result of Michael's actions for the rest of my life. But I did what the girl from Virginia Tech had written: I forgave him, and my future was enlarged. It helped me discover a Missy Jenkins I never knew existed. Had I not forgiven him, I'd still be bitter today and probably never would have done any of the things I've done to help myself and other people. I would have had no desire to. I wouldn't have the mental strength to do it.

The next time you're angry at someone and think there is no way you can forgive him or her, visualize how you would feel if you were to forgive that person. Compare that feeling to the way you feel when you're angry. You'll understand how simple the choice is to forgive.

I'm not saying the forgiving part will be easy, but the choice to do it will make much more sense than the choice to stay angry. Anger can negatively affect so many aspects of your life physically and mentally. Nothing is worth that aggravation and burden. And never forget that forgiveness is not a sign of weakness. It's the exact opposite. It's a sign of strength and courage. It shows maturity. And in the end, it makes you a better person – in your eyes, the eyes of those around you, and the eyes of God.

The last lesson is that there is no greater principle to live by than God's Golden Rule: "Treat others as you would like to be treated."

It doesn't get any more succinct than that. It's so simple to say, yet so difficult to live by. We've all heard the rule. We all know what it means. And if every person thought about that rule before doing or saying anything, the world would be a perfect place. It's the summary of God's commandments. If you don't like when people call you names, don't call other people names. If you don't like when people talk behind your back, don't talk behind their backs. If you don't like getting hit, don't hit others. If you don't like people talking down to you, don't talk down to them. It all sounds easy enough, yet we all struggle to live by it.

So how do we do it? I think it's simply a matter of thinking before speaking or acting. We react. We react every day to what we read, what we hear, what we see. And we often do it without any empathy. We need to put ourselves in the other person's shoes, then decide what the right thing is to say or do. We'll find that decision becomes so much easier, and so much better – for us and, ultimately, the world around us.

When I reflect on life, I see it as being like a walk along a trail toward a final destination. The walk can be easy and enjoyable at times – on a smooth and level path surrounded by beautiful trees, flowers, and sunshine. It can also be difficult – rough, desolate, and unstable. Sometimes we come upon an obstacle during the walk that prevents us from proceeding forward. But, with hard work, faith, and patience, we will likely overcome that obstacle and be able to continue our journey. If we can't, we take a detour around it on to an unfamiliar trail.

Taking that new trail may end up making our journey longer and more challenging but, as long as it's taking us in the direction of our destination, we'll be OK. And if it's not taking us that way, we can stop and ask for directions to another trail that will. There are always people willing to point us the right way if we tell them our problem and seek their help.

I hit the most beautiful scenery along my journey on September 4, 2007, with the birth of my son. Logan Brock Smith was born at 12:10 P.M. that day, entering the world at 7 pounds, 6 ounces, and 20-1/4 inches long. Josh and I smiled a lot, and we cried a lot. It really happened. We were a family of three. I gave birth with no complications, and Logan couldn't have been healthier.

The moment I first held him I thought about how my life was almost taken from me 10 years earlier, and how lucky I was not just to be alive, but to be a mother. I've loved watching him grow and change every day. I know when I wake up each morning, he's going to surprise me with something new: his movements, his sounds, the toys he's suddenly interested in. He's like a new gift every single day. God has truly blessed us.

The journey, though, has had some rough spots as I've made my first attempts as a paraplegic mother to take care of my child.

On my first night home from the hospital, I cried. But unlike the joyful tears the day of his birth, these were tears of frustration. Picking him up from his bassinet was physically difficult. Switching him from one arm to the other to nurse him was almost dangerous because of how hard it was to keep my balance. And the challenges have continued the more he's grown. While some things get easier with time simply because of the repetitiveness, the development of his size and attitude force me to have to constantly adjust the way I do things.

For example, as a baby, he would calmly lay across my lap as I wheeled my chair to where we needed to go. But the bigger he gets, the more he's wiggles around, making it difficult for me to safely move with him in my lap. Or if I'm holding him and he gets angry, he arches his back and squirms around like many babies do. Trying to keep my balance and not lose my grip on him as he's doing that isn't an easy thing to do.

But no matter what each day brings along my trail with my son, I've stayed focused on being the best mother I can be and making his life the best I can make it. I think often, when I'm cradling him in my arms, of how close that bullet came to killing me, and how Logan would have never existed if that happened.

I've said many times that I survived that day because God had a plan for me, and I've talked about what I think the focus of that plan is: for me to use my experiences to help others. But since the birth of Logan, I've realized that plan goes well beyond me. If God hadn't let me live, Logan would not be here today. That makes me wonder what his future holds, a future that never would have existed if I hadn't survived that tragic day. Could he be President? A doctor who routinely saves lives? A teacher who positively affects thousands of children throughout his career? What trail will he take? Where will his journey lead him? What obstacles will he face? What will he experience as he works his way toward his destination?

And what exactly is that destination I've been talking about?

Well, until about 7:40 A.M. on December 1, 1997, I'd pretty much been walking the same, smooth, level, beautiful trail my entire life with my destination clearly in sight. But a minute later I faced an enormous obstacle, one that wouldn't allow me to walk that trail any longer. The detour I chose to take required a chair, a set of wheels, guidance from countless people, and a lot of physical and mental strength that I never knew I had. It's been a long, arduous detour full of ruts and barriers, but I've continued to push forward, refusing to quit and turn back. Because of my persistence and faith, this new route has turned out to be even more scenic than the original one ever was, or would have ever been, with so many more wonderful people and fantastic experiences along the way.

And the best part?

When I reach the end of this detour, I'll reconnect with the initial trail I was on before the shooting and finally be at the destination I'd originally set out for: in Heaven, with the Lord…and walking again.

Happy Trails

Life got even better when our son Logan came along. (Photo by Patrick Reddy)

Below: I have many reasons to be happy today, but none more important than Josh and Logan! (Photo by Patrick Reddy)

ENDNOTES

1   Public Papers of the President of the United States, William J. Clinton (1997) Book 2, 2 Dec 1997, www.quod. lib.umich.edu.

2   Sue Anne Pressley, "A Bible Belt Town Searches for Answers," 22 Oct. 1997, 17 Nov. 2006, www.washingtonpost. com/wp-srv/national/longterm/juvmurders/stories/ pearl.htm.

3   Michael Carneal, interview with McCracken County Sheriff's Department detective, 1 Dec. 1997.

4   *The Paducah Sun*, 2 Dec. 1997: 1A.

5   *The Paducah Sun*, 2 Dec. 1997: 1A.

6   *The Paducah Sun*, 2 Dec. 1997: 1A.

7   Lady Stearn Robinson and Tom Corbett, *The Dreamer's Dictionary* (New York: Warner Books, 1974).

8   Lady Stearn Robinson and Tom Corbett, *The Dreamer's Dictionary*, 234.

9   Lady Stearn Robinson and Tom Corbett, *The Dreamer's Dictionary*, 370-371.

10 U.S. Census, 31 Aug. 2007, 30 Nov. 2006, http:// quickfacts.census.gov/qfd/states/21/2158836.html.

11 Bill Bartleman, "Minister rejects reports of atheism," *The Paducah Sun*, 3 Dec. 1997, 1A.

12 *The Holy Bible*, New King James Version, (Thomas Nelson, 2002), 417.

13 *The Holy Bible*, New King James Version, 423.

14 *The Holy Bible*, New King James Version, 501.

15 *The Holy Bible*, New King James Version, 454.

16 James Zambroski, "Families share final moments with world," *The Paducah Sun*, 6 Dec. 1997, 1.

17 CNN News, CNN, 5 Dec. 1997.

18 Thomas Nord, "Gift from shooting victim breathes life into patient," *The Courier-Journal*, Louisville, 4 Dec. 1997, A1.

19 Leigh Landini, "Solemn notes of 'Taps' bid farewell to Kayce Steger," *The Paducah Sun*, 6 Dec. 1997, 3.

20 James Zombroski, "Families share final moments with the world," *The Paducah Sun*, 6 Dec. 1997, 2.

21 CNN.com, "Girl wounded in Paducah likely to remain paraplegic," 11 Dec. 1997, 14 Dec. 2006, www.cnn.com/ US/9712/11/paducah.presser/index.html.

22 CNN.com, "Last of Jonesboro victims laid to rest," 28 March 1998, 2 Feb. 2007, www.cnn.com/US/9803/28/ funerals.wrap.

23 "The Shepherd Center Experience," 3 March 2007, www.shepherd.org.

24 MSNBC.com, Associated Press, "Details from Colo. school shooting emerge," 28 Sept. 2006, 10 March 2007, www.msnbc.msn.com/id/15041037/.

25 MSNBC.com, Associated Press, "5th girl dies after Amish schoolhouse shooting," 3 Oct. 2006, 10 March 2007, www.msnbc.msn.com/id/15105305/.

26 Jim Adams, "Sheriff thinks boy shared shooting plan," *The Courier-Journal*, Louisville, 4 Dec. 1997, A1.

27 Michael Carneal, interview with McCracken County Sheriff's Department detective, 4 Dec. 1997.

28 nytimes.com, Christine Hauser and Anahad O'Connor, "Virginia Tech shooting leaves 33 dead," 16 April 2007, 5 May 2007, www.nytimes.com/2007/04/16/us/16cnd-shooting.html.

29 cbsnews.com, Associated Press, "Settlement in Kentucky school shootings," 3 Aug. 2000, 16 May 2007, www.cbsnews.com/stories/2000/08/03/national/ main221586.shtml.

30 CNN.com, "Kentucky school shooter 'guilty but mentally ill,'" 5 Oct. 1998, 18 May 2007, www.cnn.com/US/9810/ 05/paducah.shooting/.

31 Drs. Benedek, Weitzel and Clark, Report of Psychiatric and Psychological Evaluation, Michael Adam Carneal, report date 17 July 1998, 1.

32 Drs. Benedek, Weitzel and Clark, Report of Psychiatric and Psychological Evaluation, Michael Adam Carneal, report date 17 July 1998, 12.

33 Drs. Benedek, Weitzel and Clark, Report of Psychiatric and Psychological Evaluation, Michael Adam Carneal, report date 17 July 1998, 18.

34 Drs. Benedek, Weitzel and Clark, Report of Psychiatric and Psychological Evaluation, Michael Adam Carneal, report date 17 July 1998, 26.

[35] Dewey G. Cornell Ph.D., Psychological Evaluation, Michael Adam Carneal, report date 3 Sept. 1998, 1.

[36] Dewey G. Cornell Ph.D., Psychological Evaluation, Michael Adam Carneal, report date 3 Sept. 1998, 25.

[37] Dewey G. Cornell Ph.D., Psychological Evaluation, Michael Adam Carneal, report date 3 Sept. 1998, 28-29.

[38] Dewey G. Cornell Ph.D., Psychological Evaluation, Michael Adam Carneal, report date 3 Sept. 1998.

[39] Diane H. Schetky M.D., Forensic Re-evaluation of Michael Carneal, report date 27 May 1998, 11.

[40] Videotape, Commonwealth v. Michael Carneal, Case 97-CR-350, 16 Dec. 1998.

[41] Videotape, Commonwealth v. Michael Carneal, Case 97-CR-350, 16 Dec. 1998.

[42] Diane H. Schetky, M.D., Forensic Re-evaluation of Michael Carneal, report date 27 May 1998, 12.

[43] Dewey G. Cornell Ph.D., Psychological Evaluation, Michael Adam Carneal, report date 3 Sept. 1998, 8-10.

[44] CNN.com, Jefferson County, Colorado Sheriff, The Columbine High School Shootings," 25 May 2007, www.cnn.com/SPECIALS/2000/columbine.cd/frameset.exclude.html.

[45] Michael Carneal, interview with McCracken County Sheriff's Department detective, 1 Dec. 1997.

[46] The White House, Office of the Press Secretary, "Interview of the President by ABC *Good Morning America*," 4 June 1999, 29 May 2007, http://clinton4.nara.gov/WH/New/html/19990604.html.

[47] The White House, Office of the Press Secretary, "Interview of the President by ABC *Good Morning America*," 4 June 1999, 29 May 2007, http://clinton4.nara.gov/WH/New/html/19990604.html.

[48] murraystate.edu, Murray State University, copyright 2000, 29 May 2007. www.murraystate.edu/secsv/hous/rdjob.html.

[49] millionmommarch.org, "How we started," copyright 2006, 30 May 2007, www.millionmommarch.org/aboutus/2000march/.

50 CNN.com, Associated Press, "Pat Morita, 'Karate Kid's'
Mr. Miyagi, dies," 25 Nov. 2005, 1 June 2007, http://
www.cnn.com/2005/SHOWBIZ/Movies/11/25/obit.
morita.ap/index.html.

51 mtv.com, "Flipped," copyright 2007, 3 June 2007, http://
www.mtv.com/onair/flipped.

52 zoominfo.com, Office of Justice Programs News, "Efforts
of 15 leaders from across the nation recognized at National
Juvenile Justice conference," 13 Dec. 2000, 5 June 2007,
http://cache.zoominfo.com/cachedpage.

53 mswheelchairkentucky.com, copyright 2007, 3 June 2007,
http:www.mswheelchairkentucky.com/about.htm
www.mswheelchairkentucky.com/about.htm.

54 Commonwealth of Kentucky Court of Appeals, No. 2004-
CA-001534-MR, Michael Adam Carneal v. Commonwealth
of Kentucky, rendered 26 May 2006, modified 4 Aug. 2006,
2.

55 Commonwealth of Kentucky Court of Appeals, No. 2004-
CA-001534-MR, Michael Adam Carneal v. Commonwealth
of Kentucky, rendered 26 May 2006, modified 4 Aug. 2006,
4.

56 Commonwealth of Kentucky Court of Appeals, No. 2004-
CA-001534-MR, Michael Adam Carneal v. Commonwealth
of Kentucky, rendered 26 May 2006, modified 4 Aug. 2006,
4.

57 Commonwealth of Kentucky Court of Appeals, No. 2004-
CA-001534-MR, Michael Adam Carneal v. Commonwealth
of Kentucky, rendered 26 May 2006, modified 4 Aug. 2006,
14.

58 Commonwealth of Kentucky Court of Appeals, No. 2004-
CA-001534-MR, Michael Adam Carneal v. Commonwealth
of Kentucky, rendered 26 May 2006, modified 4 Aug. 2006,
1.

59 washdateline.mgnetwork.com, Sean Mussenden, Media
General News Service, "Virginia Tech: Father says victim
would have forgiven," 25 April 2007, 29 April 2007, http:/
/washdateline.mgnetwork.com.

TO ORDER THIS BOOK
I Choose to be Happy
by Missy Jenkins with William Croyle

If unavailable at your favorite bookstore,
we will fill your order promptly.

— Postal Orders —
LangMarc Publishing
P.O. 90488
Austin, Texas 78709-0488
Or order online at www.langmarc.com
Phone orders: 1-800-864-1648
Fax orders: 1-512-394-0829
Questions? E-mail: langmarc@booksails.com

I Choose to be Happy
(Paperback) U.S.A. $16.95 + $3 postage
Texas Residents add 8.25% sales tax
Canada: $19.95 + postage
For quantity discounts call LangMarc Publishing

Send _____ copies to:

Name: _____

Address: _____

_____

Check Enclosed: _____Phone: _____

Credit card: _____
Expiration: _____ E-mail: _____

LaVergne, TN USA
16 October 2009
160981LV00002BA/12/P